The Blue Book on
Homelessness

Why America Can't, Won't Fix It, and What the Rest of Us Can Do About It

By TERRY ROWAN

For Gillian H. and Adrienne L.,
whose tireless labor on behalf of
the homeless is a star in our
dark night.

CONTENTS

FORWARD

The Truth of any idea, practice, or belief, can largely be determined by the measure of its effects. The numbers of homeless persons in the United States either holds steady or grows as affordable housing becomes more problematic for a large swath of its citizens.

> Strikingly, this crisis of housing insecurity is erupting in America's richest cities. New York, whose economy soared to historic heights between 2009 and 2018, watched its shelter population swell by 72% during that time. Washington, D.C., boasts one of the country's highest median incomes; it also has the highest per capita homeless rate. Unemployment at a generational low; corporate profits have surged; the signs of growth – from new construction and consumer spending to the unbridled 'revitalization' of urban space — are everywhere. Yet, teachers, maintenance workers, supermarket cashiers, medical assistants who help sustain the cities are priced out of them. ... Extremely low-income renters ... spent 50% of their income on rent and utilities. ... Unlike earlier periods of widespread homelessness and displacement, such as during the recession of 2008, what we're witnessing today is an emergency born less of poverty than no new housing, — occurring not despite but precisely because of the economic boom.[1]

The US government has basically resigned from subsidizing low-income housing.

Most citizens are not being asked to support local efforts to find below-market housing for low-income workers and the homeless, or resist when asked.

From the federal government to the smallest villages, there is scant evidence that there are any coordinated plans to eliminate homelessness, or elected leadership to implement such non-plans, or civic visions to unite the local citizenry to eliminate homelessness. The folks who do work for the homeless, mostly care agency employees and unpaid volunteers, are underfunded; ironically, they may even inadvertently enable elected leadership to say, "See, something is being done."

These are the facts about homelessness. One ought to know the facts if one hopes to do something about changing those facts.

Today, we the people seem content to stand by while nearly a million Americans sleep outdoors this very night. For many, perhaps homelessness is just one more crisis we can't/don't seem to do much about, like gun

---

1. "The New American Homeless," by Brian Gladstone, The New Republic, 8/21/19, pp.4-5

control, fixing our broken infrastructure, stopping discrimination against immigrants and people of color, sexism, discord spewed from the highest offices of the land. This make some of us feel "(Un)Comfortably-Numb," to quote Pink Floyd.

Yet, somehow, perhaps because everything is so bleak with stasis and numbness, I have the craziest sense of optimism. I keep feeling that what the homeless and lots of other housed Americans are really hungering for is a social plan for permanent housing that is street-based, practical, well-thought-through, achievable, involving many voices, funded, and healing. A plan, accountable leadership, and a vision to unite folks in such an effort – there are lots of people ready for this to happen.

I believe there is a way to house low-income workers and the homeless right now, notwithstanding our forced acknowledgment of all the truths about our state of numbness from an informal no-housing building policy nationwide. Leonard Cohen said, "The crack is where the light gets in." He also said. "There's a crack in everything." America was never perfect, just as right at this minute we're having our usual fistfights over whether to buy more slaves, or should we set them free?

This book is about seeing where those cracks are, how to empower ordinary people to solve one serious local problem with their own heads and hearts.

Most often, when I read about some ten-year plan in such and such city about how to deal with homelessness, it suggests to me that good old American indifference is at play. Most often, homelessness, like all the other challenges facing us, is presented as a technical problem seeking technical solutions, something to be fixed, as if there is no social context for the reasons why homelessness can occur in a country that always touts itself as the richest place on earth, the city on the hill, the last, best hope for mankind. Oh, American exceptionalism, how dearly you plague us with your false dreams. This deafness to our historical and continuing social amnesia is exemplified (one among many instances) by our numerous wars on drugs initiated by generations of politicians who never seem to ask themselves (and us) two basic contextual questions: (1) How does any entity expect to control deadly drugs when we only deal with the supply side of the equation? And (2) What is wrong with our core culture when so many of our citizens seek mind-altering substances to escape such alleged happiness?

Homelessness also has a social context. Homelessness a man-made construct, not some accident of history; nor, in the hard-hearted view of free market high-priests, a just outcome owing to some personal lack in spirit and energy from "losers." What are homelessness's constituent causes? Why and how is our society structured so there is an underclass that cannot find permanent housing?

So, this little book takes a wide-angle social look at the context for homelessness, but also about how such a plan, leadership, and vision in one small city will lead to permanent housing for its homeless, along with appropriate client treatment when required, so our unsheltered neighbors can resume productive lives. This effort would heal the local community as well, for providing housing for those who desperately need it also reunites us with our own empowerment and agency to fix other social ills that beset us.

When we use the term "eliminate" homelessness, we do not mean build shelters, tent cities, camp sites, and all the other ersatz non-solutions posing as solutions. We mean "eliminating" homelessness by placing such clients, along with many low-income workers, inside permanent housing that at first blush does not seem to be there.

We, the citizens of one small city, have developed such a plan. While we are unelected, we intend to provide leadership ourselves, offering a vision to rally our fellow citizens to help. We will do this knowing in our hearts that it is not just the homeless and low-income worker who needs saving, but we the people who need saving.

Regarding homelessness, Santa Rosa, California IS America. Despite its deserved reputation as the land of invention and imaginative innovation, the US historically has had little patience for messy societal problems. We still fight over health care, retirement benefits, care for the poor and indigent, housing low-income workers, un-and under-employment, racism in our neighborhoods, violence and guns, and homelessness. On the other hand, our elected officials seem perfectly OK with cutting taxes for the wealthy, so thankfully we have that going for us.

This book is nevertheless hopeful. As many guerrilla fighters have learned over the centuries, you may have to fight on the other guys' battle field, but you can still find holes through which to slip, space to set up camp, and maybe turn the local village around. That's our work: to find housing for the homeless now, and start feeling un-numb with our neighbors.

Summer-Fall, 2019
Santa Rosa, California

PART I: AMERICA'S INDIFFERENCE TO HOMELESSNESS

The Context

On any night of the year, 2019, there are between 750,000 and 800,000 people homeless in the United States. New York City (75,000) and Los Angeles (55,000) lead the way. Latest studies show that during a year, upwards of 2.5 to 3.0 million people will suffer homelessness for at least several weeks. One paper written by a Chicago-based coalition of government agencies, care providers, and charitable foundations is a typical description of the situation:

> A precise count of homeless people is elusive. The population is transient, turns over rapidly, and is difficult to locate. Reliable assessments converge on estimates of three to four million people experiencing homelessness annually.
>
> Researcher Martha Burt of the Urban Institute reports that 800,000 individuals in the U.S. are homeless on any given night. More than 1.35 million children experience homelessness in the course of a year. According to the University of Pennsylvania Dennis Culhane, some 200,000 to 250,000 of the homeless individuals are chronically homeless.
>
> Homelessness continues to increase in every region of the country. Principal causes include a drastic decline in public investment in the creation of affordable housing, escalating housing costs in the face of stagnant or declining incomes, a rise in female-headed families living in poverty, and drastic reductions in public and private safety-net services that protect against homelessness. A focus on funding emergency shelters rather than systematic solutions allows the problem to persist.[2]

This report was written almost TEN YEARS AGO! What has changed over those ten years? Very little. The report clarifies, correctly, that the essential causes for homelessness are not personal failure but structural, largely a function of the absence of policies and practices in every locality that would preclude homelessness. More bluntly, there do not seem to be any US municipalities extant that are truly in the business of eliminating homelessness. Instead, America is in the business of officially worrying about homelessness without doing much of anything to eliminate its root causes. Homelessness is treated as an eternal processing practice. Few seem to mind that it never gets solved.

Our national mythology about personal freedom is so deeply ingrained in the culture that it took a half-century of advertising and constant negative medical reporting to even begin to change Americans' mind about

---

2. Chicago Coalition of Homeless Reform, 2010.

smoking. Citizens were encouraged by the tobacco industry to celebrate our frontier mythology (Marlboro Man) so that their choice to smoke signaled independence, frontier toughness, coolness, sexual attraction, if plainly ignoring the fact that smoking is also an expensive societal problem that we all pay for as Marlboro men go about their "choice" inhaling their self-administered poison.

This proto struggle between the mythological, individual-cum-anarchist, free-to-do-whatever he wants a la frontier-loner-behavior, versus organizing society to serve the needs of the communities of Americans, is as old as the republic. Gun advocates have amnesia about American frontier history, ignoring that most of the citizens in towns like Tombstone in 1880 forbade open-carry handguns. Why? Because most of these early settlers longed for peace and quiet, schools and churches, not street duals. We all forget it took 80 years of unnecessary driving deaths to make laws about wearing seat belts and helmets for motorcycle riders. It took a hundred years of deaths in the mines to adopt common-sense safety laws (but not really attacking black-lung disease). Today, we struggle for cultural and political oxygen against highly organized, for-profit gun manufacturers and their political allies who smother all attempts to adopt any common-sense rules about gun ownership in a country that tolerates 30,000 gun deaths a year, mass slaughters by crazy people with automatic weapons on any given Sunday afternoon. So crazy is this situation that the NRA advises us today to incorporate teachers into their upside-down world by arming teachers as the latest first-responders to madmen encroaching on their campus. That we even discuss this craziness as rational business is a sign of the prisoner (us) who has come over time and conditioning to adopt the numb passivity of his jail cell as normal life.

ROOT CAUSES OF HOMELESSNESS

False Belief: It's a personal choice.

This bromide is right out of the play-book called "The Ethos of Individualism."

The mythological idea of American individualism asserts that each human being is free to invent himself, and is thus completely responsible when things don't go so well. Americans are therefore free to starve, free to go without health insurance, free to be homeless, free to be killed by another person using one of the 300 million handguns loose in the society, free to die from over-prescribed, for-profit opioids, among a long list of such "freedoms." Seen this way, homelessness is a choice. You can be homeless, or you can choose not to be homeless. According to this theory, Nancy Reagan's suggestion that addictive drugs can be stopped easily when people "Just Say No." According to this theory, held close to the heart of American industrialists from the early 18th Century, Americans would be much better off if government just stayed out of everyone's business, and just let the rest of us be "free."

Let us not dismiss such powerful mythological, religious thinking as old news. There is a lot of projected blame from some citizens when they reflect upon the lot of others, including those who are homeless. One must remember that the inverse of blaming others for their presumably-chosen misfortunes is the hidden motive of self-congratulation for being wise enough, rich enough, educated enough, etc. to avoid such misfortunes.

The myth of individualism is deep and wide in the fiber of the culture. It is celebrated in movies, media, politics, business, and all competitive endeavors. Individualism's opposite number, those collective, societal movements that benefit the group — are held in deep disdain by those who would be inconvenienced by such distributive ideas. Free-market co-religionists argue that social movements that address the collective needs of society should be labeled with the suffix,"ism," and the two "ism's" that are the most damning are socialism and communism. Thusly labeled, many such protean efforts to help society at large often die an early political death. Why? Primarily, because any use of tax money to benefit ordinary citizens violates a cardinal tenet of the free-market religion: "You're on your own." If South Dakota, with its 980,000 people and two senators, has 40 times the voting power in the US Senate than the two senators from California, then Jeff Bezos' personal wealth of $175 billion has a lot more political sway than say, the next 10,000,000 American voters.

Free-market religious tenets insist the individual is more important than the community.

Free-market religious tenets insist 330 million Americans be viewed as individual consumers, not communities. The gun lobby completely agrees with these religious tenets, insisting that the individual's right to a semi-automatic rifle, for instance, trumps the community's right to be safe from the harm inflicted on its members when a killer is exercising his Second Amendment rights to shoot his gun in a fast-food restaurant. This craziness invents ritualized, even fetishized behaviors when we as a community must deal with the aftermath of mass murders. Since January 1, 2019, up until August 31, 2019, there have been 297 mass shootings in the US, or 1.2 a day, killing 335 Americans and injuring 1219. In all these cases, the triumph of individualism over community is ritualized as follows: elected officials announce sympathy for the victims, invite us to vigils; piles of flowers, candles, teddy bears, yellow ribbons, and notes are left proximate to the scenes of the killings; everyone sends out prayers and best thoughts. Then the funerals. High-level officials solemnly plead to "give the victims a chance to heal," so the community can "come back to normal."

"Come back to normal." What does this even mean?

What does this example have to do with homelessness? Here's how: because the individual's right to a gun trumps the greater society's right to safety, homelessness us seen by many free-market co-religionists as a personal choice trumping our common need for housing.

If only the so-called free market was free. Unregulated as it is, it's not even close to free. The markets we depend upon to trade equities are manipulated, biased, and as often as possible, tampered with through lobbying and bribery. As far as the US Congress, the Supreme Court ("Corporations are People") and the President are concerned, the individual is king, and a community exists only as signposts on a freeway.

False belief: Homelessness is not partly the fault of run-away Capitalism.

In his excellent book, Sapiens, Yuval Harari, a self-professed capitalist, calls capitalism a religion, as I have been doing. A religion, he offers, is any system of thinking that asserts laws or values that transcend human behavior. For instance, most western religions assert that there is an invisible deity that sees everything, knows everything, and will reward the good and punish the evil in an afterlife. These religions require quite a bit of faith from their followers. For one example, Harari states that many Catholics believe when the ordained priest, wearing the right vestments, and saying the exact right words over ordinary bread and wine, an event called "Transubstantiation" occurs, rendering the bread and wine into the actual body and blood of Jesus Christ. Harari says Catholics believe this transformation is not a metaphor – it's an actual physical change. He says anyone attempting to show a Catholic that the bread and wine just changed are still just bread and wine are ignoring the capacity of the mind to accept beliefs that defy scientific reality.

Harari argues that Capitalism is a religion because of its initial and continuing belief that group behavior pursuant to capitalistic practices (buying stocks, for instance) creates a transcendent outcome, i.e. "The best for the most." This belief transcends scientific analysis. It is supposed to exist a priori of any human volition. Thus, such ancillary beliefs as the "hidden hand of the market" are offered on cable shows by silver-haired gentlemen wearing $5,000 tailored suits — as rock-bottom reality. The "hidden hand" is an article of religious faith. You can't see it; it's hidden. But it performs miracles. It rationalizes all those millions of unique acts on the part of individual investors and produces a magical outcome that transcends all the humans participating in that effort.

Well, not really. What about those who game the market with insider information? What about false reporting from public companies? What about jimmied results from medical trials? What about salting the mines with gold to bilk unsuspecting investors? In other words, when were the markets in America (or, anywhere else) ever free from efforts to game the system? The answer: they were never free. Only ten-tear-olds don't know this.

Harari writes in a section called "The Cult of the Free Market":

> Capital and politics influence each other to such an extent that their relations are hotly debated by economists, politicians and the general-public alike. Ardent capitalists tend to argue that capital should be free to influence politics, but politics should not be allowed to influence capital. They argue that when governments interfere in the markets, political interests cause them to make unwise investments that result in slower growth. For example, a government may impose heavy taxation on industrialists and use the money to give lavish unemployment benefits, which are popular with voters. In the view of many business people, it would be far better if the government left the money with them. They would use it, they claim, to open new factories and hire the unemployed.
>
> The free market doctrine is today the most common and influential variant of the capitalist creed.
>
> Belief in the free market is as naïve as belief in Santa Claus. There is simply no such thing as a market free of all political bias. The most important economic resource is trust in the future, and this resource is constantly threatened by thieves and charlatans.[3]

The Republican Party, despite its minority status, has been so successful arguing free market religion for 100 years that even Democratic presi-

---

3. pp.328-9.

dents (see Bill Clinton and Barack Obama) follow that line with their own lukewarm variations. The Laffer Curve, supposedly developed in the early 1980's on the back of a napkin, argued that tax cuts to the wealthy would result in vast amounts of new taxes filling state and federal coffers from newly employed workers so those tax deficits would disappear. In not one single go-around from tax cuts to the rich has this ever come true. The latest such effort, in Kansas, fostered by a true believer in the church of tax cuts for the rich, Governor Sam Brownback, pushed through a gigantic tax cut for everyone, mostly companies. The result after two years: school budgets starved, teachers fired, social services all but stopped statewide, health care severely damaged, — problems so drastic to the corporate health of the state that conservative Kansans asked the governor to quit, and go away. They're still recovering two years later.

Nevertheless, religious beliefs die hard. President Trump proposed (and got) his $1.3 trillion tax cut for the wealthy, and 18 months later, it appears that 80% of the proceeds from those cuts for companies went into buying back their stock, not hiring millions of workers.

Why are Americans so susceptible to believe these high priests whose religious arguments benefit only the rich (themselves)? Is it because of our internalized mythologies about freedom, presumed government incompetence, individualism, and faith in the faint hope of getting rich ourselves, are masterfully manipulated by media experts? Want to scare folks who are two paychecks away from being on the street themselves? Yell "socialism" when someone proposes low-income housing projects in their neighborhoods. You can't mock God (blasphemy #1) and you can't mock the free market (blasphemy#2).

If the Catholic Church finds it hard to hold accountable those clerics who have abused and assaulted children, free market priests find it hard to ever admit manipulating their revered free market. In the aftermath of the 2008 economic crash, a direct result of offering faulty mortgages to folks whose credit was finessed to make immediate bank profits, not one banker went to jail Today, three of the five largest Silicon Valley companies (with an aggregate income larger that the GNP of France) paid no income tax in 2018. That's the free market in America, manipulated and biased as it has always been. One will remember: in Mark Twain's 1880's, the industrialists, especially railroad barons, literally corrupted 18 state houses so when bond issues were proposed to finance the construction of railroads through their states, those votes were bought and sold. Ultimately, any such bond failures back then did not inure to the wealthy barons – it was states and individuals who ended up holding worthless paper.

So, religious beliefs defy rationality, especially those beliefs cynically manipulated by its best-educated practitioners. I think we could all agree that lots of bright kids who go to Harvard Business School don't necessarily adhere to the free-market religion business, but they know a good thing when they see it. They want to get rich. If that means they go to work for Goldman Sachs to develop new algorithms to manipulate stock transactions to extract wealth they themselves did not create, well, what's wrong with that?

Therefore, mythological individualism and unbridled free-market capitalism are employed to thwart any social programs that would benefit the larger society, and efforts to replace such religious beliefs are branded as radical, communistic, unrealistic, and un-American. Iran has its religious police patrolling around to keep citizens, especially women, in line with their religious beliefs, and American's true-believer capitalists rotate on Sunday shows to brand all threats to their religious practices as anti-American. Put as simply as possible, the free market has no interest in homelessness: there's no money in it.

True Belief: The US government is essentially <u>out</u> of the low-income housing business.

Since the 1980's, the federal government has basically withdrawn from serious investment in low-income housing. Perhaps beaten down by photos of burned-out project buildings in the Bronx, New York, with the subtext being about the failure of all government to understand basic free-market tenets of how housing really works, the government no longer subsidizes affordable housing for low-income Americans. Or, maybe it's because we don't have the money? What about that? Are we the richest country that ever existed, or not? Can we afford low-income housing to begin with?

Are we wealthy? The Federal Reserve has recently released a study on aggregate US wealth. The numbers are gigantic. In 2018, the Fed estimated American owned $114 trillion of assets, including $26 trillion of housing and real estate, $26 trillion of pensions (such as 401 accounts), $22 trillion of corporate stocks and mutual funds, $6 trillion of durable goods (vehicles, appliances, furniture). Liabilities, mostly mortgages and consumer credit total about $15 trillion, leaving a net worth of nearly $100 trillion.

However, the distribution of that wealth is the rub. The net worth of the wealthiest 10% of Americans represents 70% of all the US household wealth. The top 1% grew the most in the last decade. The bottom 50% of US households has virtually no net worth – in fact, it represents less than 1% of the total wealth (liabilities canceling out assets).

The biggest aggregate loser in the last 30 years has been the middle class – those with wealth starting at the median and going to the 90th percentile. Their share of household wealth, while still sizable, has dropped from 35% to 29%.

The recent growth of populism is fueled in large part by this immense disparity in wealth, and further by the perceived loss of position, equity, and status."[4]

We're plenty wealthy as a country: it's our priorities of how to spend that money that is at stake.

This information above highlights several modern tropes that pass as formal, free-market, secular religion beliefs:
1. The wealthiest (companies and individuals) are best at knowing how to spend tax money.
2. The government should stay out of society's problems. They just make things worse. The free-market is best at solving all problems.
3. The poor are poor because of personal failures. Anyone can rise up from poverty if he so chooses.
4. Regulation of industry by government (inept academics) is always a failure.

Harari is right: free-market purists, now in the political ascendancy as never before since the Gilded Age, speak from altars of fabulous wealth. Look at us, they proclaim, we are the future. Their religious oracles speak from wealth unimaginable even by the famous barons of yesteryear: "You don't need government programs, you don't need unions, you don't need wasteful health care. What you need is to go to work for Amazon, at $15.00 and hour, with no benefits. So exciting, and you'll be free!"

Those last in line, the homeless, the ultimate losers in "Trickle-Down America," the flotsam washed up on the beach of free-market hurricanes, the avatars of America's own untouchable caste, are used as the examples of what personal hell looks like from the religion of pure free-market capitalism. Like those gigantic stained-glass windows in medieval cathedrals that were used to both educate and frighten ignorant, superstitious peasants, modern Americans look at the homeless, and shudder with fear:

"Oh God, do not let this happen to me. Get them away from me."

So, President Reagan (*"The biggest lie: I'm from the government, and I'm here to help you."*) bit at the Laffer Curve, then swallowed the tenets of his free-market co-religionists to (1) throw the mentally ill out of government-run psychiatric institutions ("Go on home. You're cured!"); (2) drastically cut back on government-sponsored home-building for low-income Americans ("Go on, now, you're finally free of government interference"); and (3) broke the Air Controller Union, a symbolic act portending the continuing government resistance to union-organizing of any type. Union membership, which, over a long haul, has significantly helped bring us all

---

4. *The Washington Post*, 5/8/19

beneficial social legislation (health care, Social Security, Medicare, some bank regulation, civil rights legislation, women's rights legislation), is currently down to 7% national membership, its lowest in 100 years.

Today, HUD may administer federal cash outlays for all kinds of social programs affecting millions of people, including the homeless, but these are remnant allocations.

Support for low-income housing has all but dried up. The free market rides high. And market-pricing for homes just doesn't pay any attention to the housing needs of 80% of its citizens. In Santa Rosa, California, if a builder wants to get out of having to observe the local soft rule of retaining 15% of any development for below-market houses, all he need do is pay a fee of $16,000 to by-pass that rule. Thus, 90% of all new housing is "market-priced," that is, available only to the top 20% of buyers.

127: Number of hours per week a person paid the federal minimum wage would have to work in order to afford rent for a median two-bedroom home in the United States.[5]

California is 3 million homes short of satisfying the needs of its existing population, much less addressing the needs of its poorest citizens. We could wait for further development of our collective consciousness via outrage, frustration, demonstrations, etc., to somehow magically coalesce around shaping new leaders and legislation that will rebuild our crumbling infrastructure, ease racial tensions, elect more women, stop illegal drug use by providing a more hopeful, optimistic view of life than many of our fellow citizens seem to be experiencing. We could do that. It could take a hundred years, too. Maybe longer. How can anyone say this? Because if you look at US economic history, the economic ruling class has never voluntarily submitted to any regulation without huge fights. Banks, Wall Street, big companies will never regulate themselves. Regulations, when they do occur every 75 years or so, are usually correctives to the accrual of massive abuses suffered at the hands of folks who really know how to dominate the political discussion.

Who can wait for the next wave of economic reform? We can see the cracks in the glass right now. We choose one thing among all the ills,— homelessness — to fix. We are stone-sober about what we are up against: institutional religious beliefs about the nature of humans (You're on your own), the nature of society (Pick yourself up by your bootstraps, like I did when my father sent me to Harvard); the nature of housing (You want a house – go earn the money to pay for it); the nature of justice (Everyone deserves a good lawyer. I have several. How about you?).

We would have to leave the church of the unregulated, manipulated

5. Source: The National Low Income Housing Coalition.

free market. We would have to rejoin the human race. We would have to face and accept our unelected but accountable responsibility to find adequate, permanent housing right now for the homeless among us. We would find the services some of the homeless need to become fully functioning again. We could do this. W believe we could do this in five years. Now, wouldn't that be something?

Media-Politics Fatigue: True Belief. Or, why do we have to keep dancing when we're so tired of it all?

One cause of depression is creating the context where a person is urged to be responsible about something when she has little control over the terms or functions of the problem.

Dear Reader, what is your advice to yourself when you:
A. Read another media story about a calf-of-ice the size of Rhode Island splits off Greenland, raising the sea level even more, which will eventually drown Miami, New Orleans, downtown New York City, etc. etc.
B. Watch another report about how Putin and his thugs are manipulating US voters while our president winks and slaps him a high-five?
C. Watch another slaughter in a supermarket, school, church, by a deranged super patriot/white-supremacist/ plain crazy person exercising his God-given rights to spray bullets on his fellow citizens over his rage about … something?
D. Watch our two primary parties: one hell-bent on privatizing everything, including our air and water, for profit's sake; and the other party passing around worry towels?
E. Reading another story about how the latest three Stanford kids invented a new company that can monetize everyone's exhales to strip the carbon dioxide to save the planet at the low cost of two cents a breath, which has Wall Street all excited?

Please, make up your own list. What exactly are we being asked to do about global warming when our own elected officials do so little to show us leadership on this question? What exactly are we being asked to do about 300 million guns floating around the country? Hey Congress: Want to depress the heck out of millions of citizens to the point of political fatigue and paralysis? *Don't provide concrete plans, don't show leadership, don't share visions that unite, and don't vote on anything.* Homelessness may be #34 on many citizens' priority lists, but nothing much is being done about the first 33, either.

DERIVATIVES: WALL STREET'S GREATEST INVENTION SINCE SNAKE OIL

One Classic Case of Gaming the System

The word "derivative" originally came from calculus. It's a mathematics term. It calculates the phases of a moving thing.

Some Wall Street financial geniuses came up with another meaning for the word in the last 20 years or so. One of their best derivatives caused the 2008 financial meltdown, placing the planet at the edge of complete financial ruin.

Those geniuses decided to create an instrument that would allow large financial institutions and wealthy individuals to "hedge" their assets by buying a new kind of insurance. Suppose some of your assets were tied to inflation rates. Rising inflation would erode your position, as would lowering inflation, too, so wouldn't it be great if you could find a way to mitigate the effect of such occurrences? Derivative funds tied to mortgages allowed investors to buy a position in those funds on margin, at no more than 10% of the actual cost of the fund; it operated like a so-called futures contract, and had the facility that whichever way the inflation went, you could still win.

In 2007-08, mortgage derivative funds were based upon an unregulated banking industry offering many home mortgages that were far beyond the buyers' abilities to repay. The free-market banks did this to collect upfront fees. Banks as a group lobby hard for these breaks, and donate vast sums to both parties to extend such privileges. This is consistent with their long-standing position that free enterprise works best when business tells government what to do (stay out of our business) while they tell government what, and what not to do. When it became apparent that many banks were going to fail (mortgage defaults on a vast scale), the feds had to move in. More than 60% of the equity in the stock market would soon disappear. As Teddy Roosevelt had done with breaking up the monopolies (early 20th Century), Franklin Roosevelt had done with banking regulations and extensive social reforms (Great Depression), and Barack Obama did by bailing out the entire banking system in 2008, Capitalism would be saved from its own excesses by three presidents who were despised by Wall Street for those very actions (although a good deal of the hatred for Obama was simply because of his skin color). At the same time, individual mortgage-holders were not saved by Obama's bailout. So, banking and Wall Street were saved, while millions of ordinary Americans were left holding the bag on upside-down mortgages. And as the New Republic article quoted earlier states, this was the real beginning our current housing crisis which apparently affects two to three times the number of "counted" homeless.

Here's what Wall Street has going for it, always and today:
- When we screw up, the feds will always bail us out. We're too big to fail.
- No one of us will ever be held accountable. Our kind don't go to jail.
- Derivatives (one example) don't do anything to produce wealth; we manipulate other people's wealth and extract fees that make us fabulously wealthy.

What do derivatives have to do with housing for the poor and homeless? Derivatives are just one example of how the financial system works, and for whom. Wall Street derivative traders may walk past a homeless person sitting on a grate in New York City trying to keep warm on a cold winter day, but as a daily focus of his work nothing could be further from that trader's mind than that homeless person, who doesn't exist in any financial sense. Toothless government assists this blindness and deafness assists by throwing most of its energy towards protecting the freedom of private finance to go its merry way. "Can we help with a tax cut?"

It's that simple.

WHAT IS HAPPENING FOR THE HOMELESS IN AMERICA?

A TALE OF TWO CITIES

Would it astound you to know that New York City spends more on sheltering its homeless that any other city in the US? More than most US cities combined? In fact, over the last ten years, NYC has spent a billion dollars to shelter its homeless. Last year alone, NYC spent $363 million for shelters. That's about $5500 per homeless New Yorker in 2018.

These expenditures are widely skewed, however: in many instances, some recipients got shelter tickets for hotels that cost the city $40,000 per person for extended stays. Many recipients averaged closer to $20,000 for extended stays.

What does a "shelter" mean in New York City? It means the recipient shows up at an office to register (again), gets his ticket for a night at a shelter. At the hotel, armory, etc., the recipient must stash his earthly goods overnight. He will be patted down: no drugs, alcohol, food, water, nothing can be brought into the room. If he tries to sneak a candy bar inside his sock and it is found, he forfeits the ticket. Ditto certainly for contraband.

He must vacate the premises by 8AM. He is on his own during the day, i.e., "free."

Five thousand of those free folks in New York City head for the subways, where they wile away their free hours sleeping, sometimes talking to no apparent listeners, annoying employed New Yorkers who paid for their ride and now must endure these unwashed untouchables.

A billion dollars. Why doesn't New York City just build permanent housing for these homeless folks? A look at any Sunday New York Times magazine will immediately tell you why: all those ads showing new 80 story buildings (23 at current count) going up in New York are filled with luxury apartments for the wealthy of the world. "Give me your tired and poor" now reads, "Bring your money here. The view way up there on the 79th floor is beautiful. You can't see any people, including homeless, from up there." On August 31, 2109, the NY Times revealed that its own study showed that the so-called "enterprise zones" included in the Trump 2017 tax relief bill as a form of encouraging the development of low-income housing (the enticement being to enjoy substantial tax breaks) were instead being exploited by wealthy investors building more luxury apartments for the uber-wealthy. We are SHOCKED, SHOCKED, to learn about this terrible revelation that the financial system, the tax system, the free-enterprise system, the mysterious hand of the market, are being taken advantage of, — gamed, if you will, — by the wealthy. SHOCKING.

So, the city of New York cannot afford a permanent solution to homeless by building their way out: land is way too valuable to waste on homeless people. Instead, New York has adopted an incredibly expensive way of never solving the problem: permanent impermanence. Shelters for all, forever and ever.

Is that a model we should follow? Does the NYC shelter model imply that homeless folks move from shelters to permanent housing after a period? Where is this evidence? The answer is NO. The numbers of homeless are growing in New York for the last ten years, as elsewhere, and for similar reasons:
1. Land in many cities is too expensive to serve the needs of low-income folks.
2. Capital moving elsewhere has been hollowing out middle class jobs.
3. Free market values preclude helping 80% of the population.
4. There remains a low interest from ordinary citizens to accommodate the homeless and low-income folks next door to them.

So, the New York City shelter example is not a good model. It's a palliative, an unending process heading nowhere, a bureaucracy that becomes its own reason to exist.

What about a small city, like Santa Rosa, California? How does it deal with homelessness?

Santa Rosa is a city of 178,000 people, situated about one hour north of downtown San Francisco. It is the largest city in Sonoma County

(500,000 population). Sonoma is one of 11 counties that ring San Francisco which rank among the top 25 most expensive counties to live in the United States. A median-priced house in Santa Rosa (1700 feet, small property) costs $650,000. You might think this means that most of Santa Rosa's citizens are wealthy. In fact, one in eight Santa Rosa citizens lives below the poverty line. The mean expenditure on housing is 32% of take-home income, but for 18% (one in six folks in Santa Rosa) that population spends 50% of their take-home on rent, which indicates thousands of local citizens are one or two paychecks away from having to leave Santa Rosa, or becoming homeless themselves. The math is stunning: that's 32,000 people!

As a result of the "Tubbs Fire" of October, 2017, over 5000 homes and businesses were destroyed, or about 6-7% of the entire housing stock. Since the fire, of all the new housing permits allowed by the city so far, 93% have gone to houses that 80% of the population cannot afford, averaging $900,000+ for a new house.

How can such a thing be happening? Is this really the Santa Rosa official housing policy?

It's not a policy, but it's what is being done. Santa Rosa, like most California cities, has adopted a weak government format, with a Board of Supervisors retaining essential power and a Mayor who is mostly window-dressing. The supervisors stand for election every four years. Most supervisors appear to be fine human beings. But they do not have a viable housing policy. Why?

First, because they defer to "market pricing," a free-market article of faith. Inasmuch as the State of California, like most of the US, is no longer in the business of building affordable housing for 80% of its population, California is 3 million homes short today in just keeping up with normal growth. One might think that with a new governor (Gavin Newsom) and a super majority Democratic Assembly and Senate, the Democrats would be speedily trying to address the homeless scandal and the plight of huge numbers of low-income Californians by underwriting lots of appropriate affordable housing bills.

You would be wrong. On the first occasion in 2019 where the Democratic majority had a vote on getting such a bill (SB 50) out of committee, which would underwrite a large-scale "in-fill building" of affordable housing near transit centers emanating from major California cities, the bill was suddenly tabled for a year (the usual burial place). Why? Because thousands of letters, phone calls, and texts reached the Democrats in Sacramento from hundreds of mayors, supervisors, and ordinary citizens, themselves Democrats, with a single message: "It would not be a good idea to place housing for low-income workers and the homeless near us. Thank you."

The governor, who had just taken office on a flaming white horse of reform, quietly went to his office to stare out the window.

Santa Rosa currently has, among its 90,000 houses and apartments, 3182 affordable rentals available (3.5%). At an average of 2 persons per rental, this covers 6400 people. Since 12% of the current population lives under the poverty line ($15-25K per annum), three out of four local citizens below the below-poverty line do not have adequate housing opportunities available to them.

What's really happening in Santa Rosa is two things:
1. Many more than two occupants are squeezing into these rentals; and
2. The large majority of these folks, plus several economic layers above them (like teachers, construction workers, social workers, retail workers) are traveling long distances to work in Santa Rosa.

Today, only one in four households poor enough to qualify for rental assistance actually receives it. In a country where vital aid is treated as a lottery, families struggling to pay rent are, with few exceptions, left to fend for themselves.[6]

The big fact here is that supervisor reliance on market pricing is not a viable housing policy for more than 80% of the population. Not viable = not sustainable. The average teacher in Santa Rosa needs to travel one hour twice a day to retain her job in Santa Rosa.

So, lacking an overall housing plan, what else does the government of Santa Rosa do about the worst off, the homeless? The supervisors allocate between $2 and $3 million through care agencies to address all homeless issues for shelters, treatment, outreach, food, clothing, consultations, overhead for the agencies, etc. Does this work, in any sense of that word? One indicator would be how many folks who were formerly homeless are now housed, in 2018? Unfortunately, no one can report any such numbers. You can't find such statistics published by anyone – the city or the agencies. The best guess from 2018 is that under 100 individuals who had been homeless somehow got permanent housing. What we do know is the current number of homeless, around 2,000, has stayed mostly the same over a ten-year period. The City of Santa Rosa passed a resolution to eliminate homelessness five years ago. Having no metrics, that resolution is hardly mentioned at public meetings today.

The supervisors in Santa Rosa do not have their collective heads in the sand. In 2017, they voluntarily invited an independent consulting firm, *HomeBase*, Inc., to examine the whole delivery system for services to the

---

6. Ibid, New Republic, p.6

homeless, and to advise the supervisors as to how they might streamline the process and deliver better results. *HomeBase* interviewed 150 stake-holders, from care agency personnel to homeless persons, government officials and business people, and citizens. They pored over budgets, al-locations, systems, computers, software, communications protocols, out-reach, food banks.

HomeBase issued its report in September, 2017. Their major findings have already been alluded to in reference to the general lack of services for the homeless everywhere:
- There was/is no formal plan in Santa Rosa to eliminate homelessness.
- No one among the government agencies or care agencies is ac-countable for results. No one by name is responsible for homeless-ness as policy or practice.
- There was no effort to engage the public with an over-arching vision of how the homeless, low-income persons, struggling lower-mid-dle-class workers, were all connected, and how a comprehensive building plan might address these many citizens.

Added to the passive default by the supervisors to high-end-builders, who constantly argue there is no money in building low-income apartments or houses, and resistance from home-owners to any mention of placing such housing near to their own neighborhoods, the supervisors have a long pattern of finessing the whole homeless problem by expressions of sincere concern for their well-being while, at the same time, consistently sidestepping fixing the homeless problem as a political third rail. As a practical matter, Santa Rosa, like New York City, also offers shelters for the homeless, but only for 400 for the 2,000 people that daily call our streets home. Those homeless who do not avail themselves of shelters sleep in doorways, empty buildings, impromptu camps, tent villages. Some, who still have cars, assemble nightly in semi-safe areas where they can look out for one another more easily.

Santa Rosa also spends $9 million to reimburse the city jail for housing homeless who have been picked up for one kind of infraction or anoth-er. On any night of the year, one-third of all the prisoners in our jail are homeless people. The supervisors, all good people, would strenuously deny they were criminalizing homelessness. They maintain they are trying hard to deal with the problem with limited resources and muted support from taxpayers.

Santa Rosa also reimburses $7 million to local hospitals for emergency ambulances and treatments for homeless people.

It could be suggested that the $16 million to jails and hospitals is mon-ey out the barn after the door is closed. Also, that the $2-3 million to the care agencies to perform all these complex services is vastly inadequate to the task.

In all these ways, Santa Rosa is like California writ large, like New York, like the country, when dealing with homelessness. There is little will anywhere to tackle the problem, little political energy to lead and take responsibility, and little risking of vision to unite low-income workers, middle class workers, and the poor, and the homeless together into a seamless population, called "US."

Reminder: You can't get optimistic about seeing the light coming through the cracks until you've learned the truth about the situation at hand.

PART II: NIMBYism AND ITS CAUSES

QUESTIONS WE ASK OURSELVES

What's at the bottom of all this resistance from local homeowners to any mention of low-income housing abutting their neighborhoods?

There are lots of opinions on why there is so much resistance among people who ought to know better regarding the prospect of housing for the homeless, otherwise referred to by some as having your neighborhood invaded by a horde of "zombies."

"Zombies." That's one of the many terms you can hear at meetings called by any elected official brave enough to suggest there are benefits of placing a three-story, eighty apartment complex in the neighborhood that will offer below-market rates for its tenants. "Zombies, losers, addicts, drunks, criminals, takers, lazy, rapists," and so on from half the assembly; the other half, stunned into silence at the anger of neighbors they thought they knew.

We decided to drill down and conduct six focus groups in Santa Rosa and its local communities to learn more nuanced reasons why some neighbors feel these ways, and whether there were any opportunities to find common ground and work together?

We tried to observe the local demographics on income, race, ethnicity, age, and so on.

We learned a lot about our Sonoma neighbors. Our primary findings:

1. Property values were obviously a big issue. There were several participants in every focus group who explained their families had bought the house they were living in, many years ago for a modest sum.
   Such bungalows in Santa Rosa feature two to three bedrooms inside a 1500 sq. ft. footprint, with a small back yard. But 40 years later, that little house was now worth $645,000. The present owner, late middle age, was going to retire from his construction job in a few years. He was counting on the appreciation from the sale of his house at the time of sale to be the main support for his retirement. He was sorry to say that the prospect of one of those "Bronx-type" massive apartments for low-income workers, and the homeless, would depress his home value, and that possibility he took very personally.

2. Class resentment was present at a low boil. Several participants at different meetings said words to this effect: "I don't care what anyone says about how wonderful such a building will be, because who can you really trust? I know the people who build it, the politicians who want it, do not live in my neighborhood. And mostly I know that no politician will ever propose such a fix for the homeless

in a wealthy neighborhood. That's just the truth." Many participants nodded their heads in agreement at these comments.

It's hard to argue with this insight about class, isn't it? In nine years living in Santa Rosa, I've never heard any supervisor even breathe a thought about asking a wealthy neighborhood to share in this kind of venture to help the homeless.

3. What's in it for them? It's never explained how such proposals for building a multi-level building keyed to low-income housing benefits the local neighborhoods asked to support them. Why doesn't someone from government take the time to clearly explain what the neighborhood gets out of such a proposal, should it advance to completion? Unless, there is nothing the locals get out of it.

4. What about normal fears that certain formerly homeless clients who might live in the neighborhood will continue to suffer from psychological, physical, or addictive pathologies and might not be in treatment? Or worse, they need treatment but refuse it! What is the local neighbor entitled to know about this client?

Lots of legitimate issues, yes?

Suppose someone tried to respond to the legitimate concerns of many homeowners at the prospect of living next to one or more homeless persons? Suppose there were some reasonable answers to these concerns that might calm a rational mind?

Such answers might count if homelessness, per se, were a rational subject. When discussed by academics, it is rational. But as experienced by the homeless themselves, and their prospective neighbors, it's hardly a rational thing. It's quite personal, upsetting, disorienting for many. Why?

One will remember the old issue of busing children to racially integrate public schools. As far as busing being an academic formulation, it made total sense on paper, at least to those who believed in the moral virtue of integration. It might even have seemed to these academics and their well-meaning, allied politicians to be a way of solving two things at once: (1) get the white and black kids to mix at early ages and, (2) when they're older, those kids are already sensitized to what integration feels like. Viola, integration of the races. That this possible formulation forgot that nine tenths of the social construct outside schools remained segregated – housing, access to jobs, systematic racism, — was understood in retrospect. Should integrating public schools have been the tail wagging the dog on systemic racial segregation?

But today's systematic racism and its political instruments — terrorism (historical lynching or racial-motivated shootings today), Jim Crow laws suppressing voting among people of color, red-lining black areas by banks to deny loans or charge higher rates, jury nullification (refusal to uphold the law of due process), de facto segregated schools, which of course still exists in every state in the Union to this day, all help us understand how deeply ingrained such prejudicial practices can be.

It's easy to criticize the busing strategists of the 1960's, after the fact. But how about our own contemporary racism? What busing helped ironically achieve was (1) "White Flight" occurring in hundreds of cities to the suburbs across the US; (2) Nixon's "Southern Strategy" immediately began to peel off resentful white Southern Democrats. (3) The "Willie Horton" dog-whistle ads showed up regularly in national elections (still do). (4) Hypocrisy also leavened that busing bread: Ted Kennedy, the main sponsor of such legislation, sent his own children to segregated private schools.

But change does come to America. Despite everything that's so wrong, and perhaps because of what's so wrong, the society nevertheless does change slowly, adjusts and moves on regarding important social questions. I cite gay marriage and trans-gender rights as two huge social changes in progress. It's still hard to know whether all the current surfacing of racism is a sign of honest reckoning or incipient rabid hatred bubbling up, or possibly both at the same time. It's also hard to spot heroic myth-busters who speak with a common touch to give voice to workable solutions for so much that plagues on our human progress: income distribution gone crazy, no infrastructure repairs, no housing for so many, health care so stressfully argued, and so on.

One must always remember that technical innovation is what America eats for three meals a day, but social innovation is very hard for us. There's an American human being killed by a hand gun every 16 minutes, every day of the year. One must have happened during the writing of this paragraph.

Do local neighbors have a right to know all about the medical, emotional, or psychological condition of a homeless person renting next door? Homeless people, like all of us, are protected by law from having his personal medical information broadcast over the neighborhood. But gosh, don't free-minded, fair-thinking neighbors have some rights too? What if this guy Bill is an alcoholic, a drug addict, a child molester, a thief?

Does it matter that the Sonoma CDC reports that approximately 35,000 of the 500,000 Sonoma County resident population (7%) are alcoholics? Or that another 7,000 individuals are using illegal drugs recreationally or from habitual use and need? Probably not, because the strange thing about housed alcoholics, or drug addicts, is that most of these addicted folks are employed, and live otherwise quiet (if desperate) lives next door. In most instances, these addicts are not always noticed outside those families. Regarding child molestation and theft, all such convictions are a matter of public record.

What is the difference between the family next door that harbors an alcoholic member quietly, and the formerly homeless person who is placed under medical care next door who may also be an alcoholic? The big difference is not one of academics, but feelings. The local addict is family, and love him or not, family is family. Bill, the outsider homeless person, however, wears the bad guy hat in this story: not family. So, God knows what this guy is capable of, right?

Placing homeless persons in empty bedrooms presents one viable, available, direct way to house lots of folks without necessarily dealing with all the permits, time, money, or BIG solutions insisted upon by government for multi-use buildings proposed for low-income workers and the poor in local neighborhoods. But, how to do go into local neighborhoods with programs for social change in the biggest sense of that word, "Doing Good," but also finding out what the neighbors get out or it? If the solution to any housing plan doesn't include the locals, forget trying to get their cooperation. That was the single biggest find in the focus groups: if you want the locals to open their hearts, work with you, help solve a vexing social problem, you better know what they want out of that proposition. That's only fair.

For one hundred years, accession to the middle class has come not through accruing capital from salary, but the return on capital on investment in housing. Property ownership is a big distinction and indicator of American virtue. That drunk next door may be a personal mess, but if his lawn is cut and the house is painted, I'm not going to worry about him so much.

"Bill, on the other hand, that homeless guy they sneaked next-door under our noses, he doesn't own property. He has no stake in this neighborhood. Why would he give a fig what happens in this place; it means nothing to him. For all we know, he could be a bomb ready to go off."

In the first Batman movie, Jack Nicholson, playing the Joker, is threatened by Bruce Wayne. Just before he shoots Wayne, he says, "Never rub another man's rhubarb."

The local guy's rhubarb in Santa Rosa is his house's sale price. You'd better not mess with it. Same in Omaha, Nebraska, Ames, Iowa, wealthy San Francisco.

Even when an agency places a homeless person in an empty residential bedroom with the owner's consent, and rent is guaranteed, and appropriate care is arranged for the client and disclosed to the landlord, plus a legitimate, standard rental contract is executed, and rules of the house are established and understood by client and owner, and finally a work training plan is set up for the client, what could go wrong with the neighbors?

Lots could go wrong. Finding available rooms for homeless people (a good idea) is easily trumped by irrational fears of some neighbors (bad idea) that should not be underestimated, or possibly assuaged by any disclosures of, heaven help us, big meetings.

I asked this kind of question in the latter three focus groups of all the participants. The answer I generally heard was: "Yes, we know there are alcoholics and drug addicts in our neighborhood, but they're our addicts. They keep their houses neat, they go to work even when they're making a mess of their private lives. But this stranger, this outsider, we don't know anything about him. He doesn't own property here, he has no connection to us, so how can we trust that situation? Better to Just Say No."

So, property ownership is a big distinction and indicator of American virtue. Homeless people are presumed to have no such virtue, and thus they may be viewed as stateless persons, not "real" Americans.

This is why the outsider, the one with no stake in the neighborhood, the property-less homeless person, who may also have some adaptive responses to trauma that include alcoholism and other addictions, is a persona-non-gratis for a lot of neighbors. To their way of thinking, rejecting the homeless out of hand is not being nasty, prejudiced, or hateful; instead, they're just protecting their twenty-five-year effort at husbanding their major (and maybe only) financial asset from possible ruination.

Therefore, a strategy for how neighborhoods must be approached to place homeless folks inside empty bedrooms (and other alternatives) is not just a technical issue. It's a human social issue of the first importance. Look around: Where, in the whole of America, do you see any major success stories for neighborhood organizing efforts to end homelessness? Of course, such efforts must exist, but they're hard to find. And what does change look like inside these neighborhoods?

The way private companies make decisions that affect individuals and neighborhoods without consulting the neighbors is to frame their changes as "progress." because all Americans have been conditioned to internalize the assumptions of free enterprise until it has become the state religion. For just one example, Duke Energy has probably done more to ruin the environment in West Virginia than any other entity in history, including the Ice Age. They have stripped off the tops of mountains, polluted rivers and streams with toxic run-off, dumped heavy metals into the soil, closed mines and broken strikes, all in the name of "progress." Moreover, such awful behaviors pale next to free enterprise's greatest triumph: getting workers to vote against their own interests year after year by branding government as the true enemy of "progress." Cigarettes, alcohol, gun sales, tax breaks or mining coal — instead of investing in health care, — onwards goes the eternal business campaign to convince workers government is the enemy.

Repeat: Don't rub another man's rhubarb and mess with state religion.

So, now we know what we're up against. It isn't just finding empty rooms to house the homeless as a technical item, but more importantly making a serious effort to understand how local folks already relate to the outsider (the homeless), and how we get in their heads and hearts to start that change process.

Because what else is available to us? We either leave the million homeless where they already are, uncared for, this shame and blot on our collective humanity, or we wait for politicians to assume responsibility they are reluctant to do. As one Southern senator once confided, "There is no punishment for doing nothing."

We start in one small city, assume the responsibility as unelected but accountable citizens, develop our own local plan to house the homeless, accept and broadcast our transparency, advertise our vision of bringing home our brothers and sisters inside the community, and show ourselves to still have some agency to produce change and peace by rallying as many citizens to do what is right.

A short review of the structural, cultural, mythological restraints causing inaction across America to end homelessness:

- An internalized and projected belief that homelessness is a choice — victim blaming.
- An internalized belief in the myth of individualism: the homeless person is an avatar of irresponsibility looking for a handout.
- Religious belief that the unregulated free market (not government) is best at solving all social, economic, and political problems.
- The false belief that accrued value of sale price of home is threatened by the re-introduction of homeless persons to the neighborhood, even one by one.

In the wilderness, Buddha ate beetles, snails; caked his body with mud; slept under bridges. He meditated for years on the sublime indifference of the universe as the great orbs rotated endlessly from some original impetus that has no memory. He saw the moon had no choice but to follow the earth. He understood that every animal on the earth followed ancient behavioral prescriptions over which they had little volition. One day he felt a blaze of light course through his body. A voice spoke to him:
  "Get off your ass and do something."

Questions we ask ourselves contemplating how to organize local neighborhoods to be more accepting of the tired, the poor, the homeless yearning to be housed:

1. Where would housing for the homes among us come from if the US government is essentially out of the home-building business for low-income workers and the poor?
2. Given the historical importance of home value to average homeowners, how can their fears of being financially threatened by accepting homeless into their neighborhoods be ameliorated?
3. Who would do this organizing work and how would that work be funded?
4. How long would it take to eliminate homelessness locally while acknowledging the lack of local, state and governmental support, pushback by spontaneous neighborhood resistance, and the weight of long-time judgment, disdain, and hostility to helping the least among us, by the many?
5. Who really benefits from the scarcity of housing?

The author(s) of this proposal have spent three years studying homelessness on a national, state-wide and local basis. We have read hundreds of scholarly reports on the matter. We have visited homeless programs in three states to date, spoken with tens of valiant volunteers who have given a decent portion of their lives to trying to solve this vexing problem. We have met many local homeless persons, interviewed them often, discovered and recorded their personal stories, and learned the complexities of the human drama of this trauma writ large on our streets.

We deeply recognize the layers of need among the homeless that are reflected only partially by their absence of housing. We do not underestimate how such an effort to house 2,000 local people in Santa Rosa, arrange proper care for them over an extended period, follow up with training and counseling, will require in hours, effort, financing, and spiritual energy. The city of Santa Rosa spent somewhere in the vicinity of $20 million in 2018 on direct care ($2-3 million) for the homeless, and indirect reimbursement for jail time ($9 million), $7 million reimbursement to hospitals for emergency medical care, and perhaps $1 million in emergency response to urgent requests.

We believe we have a strategy that could permanently house and care for all 2,000 current homeless persons for that same $20 million, but distributed over five years. We see a way to house those folks right now without resorting to ten-year programs to enlist high-end builders and reluctant politicians. We believe we know how to raise initial funding independent of the city and county. We believe we understand how to recruit a small army of unpaid but vital volunteers to conduct much of the neighborhood organizing. We believe we understand how to message such a sustained effort via professional advertising, and how to conduct continuous local (small) meetings to listen and acknowledge local fears about "the stranger among us," and how to further recruit many of these neighbors in the overall effort to solve homelessness.

We may require some refinement about our assumptions and funding, but we are not naïve, young (sadly), idealistic, or heroes. Mostly, we are just tired of driving past hundreds of untouchables every day in our streets.

Untouchables, like Olian Byrd.

OLIAN BYRD: THE STORY OF A "FIXTURE"

On a cold and rainy night in late January, 2017, an anomalously wet winter in the midst of five-year drought, Olian Byrd was brought to a local Santa Rosa hospital after a stranger had passed his makeshift street tent, and was unable to get any response from Mr. Byrd.

Mr. Byrd was declared dead at the hospital. He had suffered a massive heart attack, and was also said to have frostbite on his left foot. He was 62 years of age.

Olian Byrd was born in Santa Rosa, went to schools there, graduated from Santa Rosa High School where he had acted in plays. He attended the local junior college for some courses but left without finishing a degree. He was a handsome young man with an affection for nice clothes, a smile that lit up a room, and a friendly disposition. He had developed a great talent for ice skating along the way, and was so good on the ice he turned professional and danced in several ice shows in the US and Europe.

He met a local girl, they married and over the next few years had three children. Olian worked at several jobs in Santa Rosa. By all appearances, he seemed a happy, productive person, if drifting a bit regarding a solid career.

Then, in his late twenties, a shadow descended over Olian Byrd. He began to hear voices talking to him. He ignored these strange visitations as best he could until he was distracted and disturbed much of the time. The voices began to interrupt normal life, including work places, so that his behavior alerted supervisors and shoppers that something might be seriously wrong with Olian. Once, he pretended to be a traffic police-person until he was stopped directing traffic at a busy street intersection. He was fired from a succession of jobs. His young wife was naturally very upset with this onset, urged Olian to get professional help, which he was reluctant to do, a pattern that would persist for much of his adult life.

Then, in his thirties, Olian left his wife and children and turned to the streets. He had no means of income, was medically undiagnosed, had scant belongings, and had abandoned the one solid support he did have, his family, who were devastated.

Life on the streets: pushing one's belongings around in a "borrowed" shopping cart, eating at food banks, sleeping under bridges and in doorways, rarely having a shower or seeing a doctor, alone with one's thoughts, or, in the case of Olian Byrd, never alone from the constant chatter in his head from many voices.

Olian did encounter the care agencies now and again. Several knew him; one or two had tried to keep him around long enough to get him diagnosed. Sometime in those first ten years away from his family, Olian was indeed diagnosed with acute paranoid schizophrenia. But treatment from understaffed, underfunded agencies, coupled with Olian's resistance to being tied down anywhere, or taking prescribed meds, resulted in his being mostly left alone. One will remember that most of the mentally ill had been released from state hospitals in the 1980's and 1990's as the federal government tightened, then shut off, nearly all its aid for such institutions. Olin Byrd was "free."

So, Olian Byrd lived on Santa Rosa's streets as a seriously-ill homeless person who was essentially untended by any institutional care system, for twenty-five years.

Several years before his death, he found a place which he decided to make his permanent camp. It was a patch of grass at the edge of a Shell gas station at the corners of Industrial and Cleveland Avenues in northwestern Santa Rosa. He had the use of the bathroom at the gas station, and most often, the clerks who came and went at the cash office treated Olian to coffee and something simple to eat for breakfast. He sat in an old aluminum chair under a large California oak tree, and still occasionally flashed to passersby that famous smile of the young man he had once been.

How many people passed by that corner each day? Traffic studies indicate that perhaps as many as 13,000 vehicles pass those corners daily. A lot of eyes saw Olian Byrd for many years. It is certain some passersby stopped to hand him some coins, or perhaps an unfinished sandwich. It's just as certain that many thousands of eyes never really saw him, virtually invisible to perhaps indifferent hearts and eyes.

It was disclosed after his death that his wife and kids never forgot him. He had been the recipient of a small bank account set up by his wife years before upon which he could draw small amounts of money. But of all the ironies, on the very day he died, one of his daughters filled her car with gas at that corner Shell gas station, not recognizing that the man in the rain-slicked chair fifty feet away was her long-absent father.

How does a man get frostbite in Santa Rosa, one of the jewels in beautiful Sonoma County, that place where yellow mustard plants wave on hillsides in spring, only to be replaced by thousands of cultivated acres of green grape plants pushing up this year's crop of delicious reds and whites? Frostbite, the kind that results in amputated limbs if left untreated, was literally what Olian had. There are probably very few people around who romanticize homelessness, but contracting frostbite because of the cold and wet weather should disabuse any such romantic notions of what life on the street is really like.

The day after Olian Byrd's death, his story landed on the first page of the local Sonoma paper, the Press Democrat. The writer referred to Olian as a town "fixture," and certainly in the light of his long-term presence on the streets, this was possibly a descriptive word. But in the context of his sad life and desperate death, it is an inadvertent damning word as well, for a fixture is something so ordinary in the environment that we may take it for granted, or no longer even see it. A fixture who is a human being dying alone at night on our streets ought to be a light in our collective hearts that we all allowed this to go on, one might think.

Was Olian Byrd "free" to live on the streets this way? Apparently, yes, except when his presence was annoying for some reason, and then he might spend a night in jail. In our current possibly warped sense of values, a mentally ill person's election to live and die on the streets is apparently equal to our collective indifference. A "Whatever, Dude," relationship.

What did the police and hospital do with Olian's scant belongings? The inventory of flotsam in a typical homeless person's shopping cart would not be fought over at a will reading: soiled, greasy clothes, tarps to keep out bad weather, a tattered sleeping bag, some old paperbacks and newspapers, crushed water bottles, outer clothes, candy bar wrappers. What do the police and hospitals do in most cases with such flotsam? It ends up in a dumpster, the same way the body of a homeless person with no family claimants might end up in a potter's grave at the county's expense, with no marker to say this was a person, a human being, someone who once danced in plays, and ice skated, and loved a wife and children.

If Olian Byrd's marker were on our own foreheads, maybe it would read: "Whatever, Dude."

Every one of the two thousand homeless persons in Santa Rosa today has a story. Every one of us can say, "For Heaven's sake, isn't this why we pay our taxes, don't we have poor houses," except those lines were spoken a long time ago by Ebenezer Scrooge. But Scrooge, as we all know, came around to his hopeful, generous heart just in time to redeem his life.

That's our chance, too. If we take it.

PART III: VISION, PLAN, LEADERSHIP

How Does a Town Take Responsibility for Housing its Own?
What's the vision?
What's the plan?
Who is the leadership?
How does the project get funded?
How long does it take to house 2,000 people?
How do we measure success?

THE VISION

What ethical, moral vision informs the effort on the part of local citizens to fix the crisis in housing for the homeless and others affected by little low-income housing to speak of in northern California? (or, you pick your own town), given these accurate, descriptive findings:

- The federal government and the states, including California are out of the business of supporting low-income housing for lower middle class, low income workers, the working poor, and obviously, the homeless. The absences of housing policies addressed to low-income workers and the homeless are unsustainable. Official statements of concern for the homeless do not constitute a housing policy.
- The federal government and the states, including California, are essentially lukewarm about the care of homeless trauma treatment business. Their ready answer to such a charge is to point to a myriad of (underfunded) programs that ostensibly address all such pathologies. The counter to that argument is to point to thousands upon thousands of untreated persons in the state and local communities who daily wander the streets.
- Local government reliance on care agencies to carry out treatment of the indigent is a case of cutting off the fingers on the helping hand. Every care agency supported by state and local funding is so starved that budget restraints dominate their working lives. These folks do magnificent, and often unappreciated tasks on behalf of us all. Underfunding does not make a policy.
- Fear of asking local citizens to share in solutions regarding helping the indigent is the third rail of political life.
- The proposition that worrying about the re-sale value of one's home, precluding concern about homeless neighbors is true for some, perhaps forever, but not true for all by any means. Finding and cultivating those citizens who are willing to help is our essential work.

Words like "Vision" can stir up sentiments of nobility and transcendent calling. Our vision is much more prosaic:

1. Find and present ways and means for local neighbors to participate in the determination of how the homeless and low-income workers might be housed in their neighborhood.
2. What's in it for them? Put them in the profit-making business as landlords.
3. For those who are unable to offer empty bedrooms and other accommodations for tenants, train those neighbors to assist and support landlords and tenants who can and will offer bedrooms.

It's simple: government is not going to help for a considerable period. High-end builders will continue to ignore housing projects for 80% of the population. Fixing homelessness is up to the rest of us. We can maintain the value of our houses, make some extra income now, and control the growth of our neighborhoods in ways that meet our common needs and desires.

HOW TO MAKE A PLAN

A recent, typical letter to the editor of the *Press Democrat*, Sonoma County's largest newspaper:

> *Bowing to Nimby's*
> *Once again, Santa Rosa's City Council bows to NIMBYism of Santa Rosa's citizenry, which mouths words of caring for those displaced by fire or other circumstances but doesn't want to make an iota of sacrifice to actually help them ("Council hits pause on renter protection", Wednesday). The latest example — the delay in adopting an anti-discrimination ordinance because property owners whined about not being consulted enough – is a travesty and belies the City Council's oft-expressed but little acted-on concern for increasing housing for the homeless. We can — and must — do better.[7]*

Announcing the Official Santa Rosa City Council Kabuki[8] Dance Rules of Homeless and Neighborhood Relations:

1. The City Council regularly instructs the police to conduct sweeps of impromptu encampments of homeless people in Santa Rosa. The

---

7. N.O., Sebastopol

8. A Kabuki dance is an ancient Japanese artistic tradition of carefully structured moves that pleases the eye, and reassure a sense of tradition and stasis. When you watch Kabuki dancers, you do not expect innovation: no head-spinning, splits, rap poetry, originality. You do expect tradition, done with exquisite care and polish. Kabuki dance classes held for aspiring politicians are held every Wednesday.

police are instructed to remove tents, confiscate all unattended property and personal items, and to cart them away. The areas are hosed down. Resisters can be arrested or cited. The police call these exercises "turfing," a term meaning "Kicking the can down the road." Many police have been quoted as saying they hate these exercises, and see no social benefit to them. Why are they done anyway? Whom do such exercises benefit? If not the homeless, who?

2. The City Council members do not ask, dare not ask, any local citizens to sacrifice anything, or even address, the homeless crisis, or the general dearth of low-income housing projects.

3. Individual Supervisors holding press conferences uniformly espouse bromides of concern, caring, attesting to their constant attention to this complex, vexing problem (homelessness), but somehow never come up with any substantive program to lessen or eliminate homelessness.

Compare to New York City

Let's look at New York City. They have 75,000 homeless people in their streets. What are they doing?

New York City spends more money on shelters than any place on the planet – more than a billion dollars in the last ten years. NYC shelters 95% of its homeless. Why doesn't it build permanent housing with those dollars? Because NYC is out of that business. Because land in NYC is now 95% dedicated to high-risers for the wealthy and very rich.

Shelters are, by definition, an impermanent non-solution to a serious social problem. A municipality that wants to solve the homeless crisis will not choose a temporary non-solution to nowhere. However, if you see homelessness as an eternal process without solution, then shelters are perfect. "New York has opened 23 new homeless shelters since 2017 and has 20 more in development. It has poured more than $80 million since 2014 into new centers, outreach programs and specialized services specifically aimed at homeless people on the street, including the creation of a database that helps outreach workers identify and track individuals by name.

It has also taken more punitive steps. Police officers have handed out a flurry of civil summonses to try and clamp down on disruptive behavior on the subway. Currently, between 1,600 to 1,800 summonses per week are issued prohibiting transit conduct – Including jumping turnstiles, stretching out in subway cars and on platforms, smoking and drinking alcohol … .[9]

---

9. *NYTimes, June 27, 2019, p.a23*

Or, NYC has added another level of bureaucracy without adding the resources that are needed to help people get off the streets. This approach is packaged with a carrot and a stick: every night is another shelter-stop of temporary relief; but mess up, and you're in jail. If you want to watch terrific kabuki about the plight of the homeless, most big city mayors are among the best kabuki interpreters.

How about looking at what the Maryland's Montgomery County Council recently did on the topic of homelessness?

> The agenda said the Montgomery County Council would vote on an ordinance allowing homeowners in the county, a wealthy Maryland suburb of Washington, D.C., to create basement or backyard apartments, a modest proposal to ease the crucial shortage of affordable housing.
> The protesters who filled the front rows of the Council last week thought they knew better.
> This is not about providing affordable housing,' said Hessie Harris, a 70-year-old homeowner. 'The goal is to do away with single family communities. They claim these are going to be in-law suites and then there goes the neighborhood! They could put in flophouses.'
> 'That's where the backyard trailers are going to go,' said Dale Barnhard, one of the more than 1500 who signed a petition opposing the dramatic change in rules.
> The problem is that places like Montgomery County need big, disruptive changes to provide affordable housing for a growing population, to address economic and racial inequality and to limit climate change. The county, which has more than one million residents, a larger population than all but a handful of American cities, is increasingly unaffordable, with average housing prices soaring above $400,000. The county's employees are among those looking in from the outside. A county survey last year found that 45% of Montgomery County's 9,243 employees lived elsewhere. Richard Hoye, 63, a retired firefighter and county resident, said that included most of his former colleagues, and was more common among younger firefighters. 'Why should somebody risk their lives in a county where they can't afford to live?' he said.[10]

Familiar, yes?

Closer to home, how about San Francisco? What are they doing about their homeless population (8,000)?
    In 2019, residents of the Embarcadero are suing the city for approving a temporary homeless shelter along the waterfront. The reason: "It's the wrong fit."
    The tech industry is stepping up, thank goodness. The non-profit "All

---

10. *NYTimes*, editorial by Binyamin Appelbaum, June 8, 2109.

In" campaign sponsored by Daniel Laurie, local multi-millionaire, has raised $100 million from many local tech companies to find housing in San Francisco for 1,000 (12%) of the homeless population by 2022. Laurie's idea is to convince local landlords to rent to homeless folks and local neighborhoods to find acceptance in their hearts for this cause. It is unclear at this moment what those specific plans to soften those hearts look like. Nevertheless, privatizing homelessness to billionaires because the rest of us are unwilling to underwrite our own responsibilities, seems to be the wave of the future. Hooray for the billionaires!

As we have discussed, the flow of tech money (salaries) has driven out hundreds of thousands of lower-income workers from many US cities, including teachers, social workers, retail workers, etc. It is difficult at this precise moment to see what earthquake of consciousness is going to occur to address or reverse the avalanche of money driving housing pricing ever skyward in San Francisco. It's an unsustainable trajectory, but what will stop it?

And what about these NIMBY's, anyway? Are they conservatives blocking any kind of social program that interferes with their free market religion?

Not exactly. In another *NY Times* editorial by Farhad Manjoo entitled "Nimby Liberals Make Cities Unlivable," he states that when cost of living is included in the analysis,

California ranks as the most poverty-stricken state, with a fifth of its population struggling to get by... . The problems of affordable housing and homelessness have surpassed all superlatives – what was a crisis is now an emergency that feels like a dystopian showcase of American inequality.

Look at San Francisco, Nancy Pelosi's city. One out of every 11,600 residents is a billionaire, and the annual household income necessary to buy a median-priced home now tops $320,000. Yet the streets there are a plague of garbage and needles and feces, and every morning brings fresh horror stories from a "Black Mirror" hellscape. Homeless veterans are surviving on trash from billionaires' mansions. Wealthy homeowners are crowd-funding a legal effort arguing that a proposed homeless shelter is an environmental hazard. A public-school teacher suffering from cancer is forced to pay for her own substitute.

And at every level of government, our representatives, nearly all of them Democrats, prove inadequate and unresponsive to the challenge at hand.... California lawmakers used a sketchy parliamentary maneuver to knife Senate Bill 50, an ambitious effort to undo restrictive local zoning rules and increase the supply of housing.

This sort of nakedly exclusionary urban restriction-ism is a particular shame of the left.

Wouldn't it be edifying to see Republican hawks and Democrat doves fighting out an election over who is tougher on poor folks – the Republicans praising efforts to separate children from parents and stuffing them into cages at the borders, while the Democrats collect money from lots of wealthy San Franciscans and New Yorkers who disdain anyone (read: "homeless, especially") from despoiling their precious neighborhoods?

Manjoo makes this point well: both conservatives and liberals want to *"preserve local character, maintain local control, keeping housing scarce and inaccessible,"* code conduct really aimed at raw exclusion as a means of maintaining high real estate costs, and profits.

Is this really true? Is housing policy in California, for one example, so blatantly biased towards the wealthy?

In separate studies of three cities in north county, Santa Rosa, Napa, and Petaluma, city figures show that of all the housing permits approved and built in these three cities since the 2008 recession, an average of 92% an of those permits disproportionately served wealthier clients.

A poem is called for:

> *Sir Conservative, we disdain your disdain*
> *for the tired and poor who come to our*
> *shores seeking surcease and ease from*
> *their travails, to find at last some peace.*
>
> *I read about this in the papers, I see it*
> *on TV, I get texts about your hatreds*
> *and urgent distinctions to keep them away.*
> *Shame on you. Have you no decency?*
>
> *Why, we have billionaires sponsoring our*
> *homeless populations. I am going to a meeting*
> *tonight to propose a perfect place to build*
> *yurts for those homeless – Death Valley.*
>
> *Hot, yes, but lots of room, and far away from here.*

Is there no example of a good and decent program for the homeless in all of North County, California? Just one example we can all look at, understand, praise, and learn from?

Yes, there is one terrific example. It's called "Homeward Bound," and it resides in Marin County, just over the Golden Gate Bridge and extending up to Sonoma. Marin has many features that distinguish it, including its small population, just over 250,000, and that it is the wealthiest county on a per capita basis in the entire US. Incidentally, Marin has maintained a nearly perfect lock against building any low-income apartments for a 40-year period. Hooray for Marin.

Homeward Bound is well-established in Marin. It owns and operates ten different houses for long-term rentals for all kinds of persons, including vets, seniors, those with medical problems, homeless young people, and so on. In addition, Homeward Bound also runs 8 family service housing locations that provide 167 beds. Total beds for homeless: 123. Homeward Bound also has three mental health service compounds providing 62 beds, and two large job training programs that accommodate up to 80 students during eight-week programs.

Homeward Bound is tightly networked into the governmental, religious, and social service agencies throughout Marin. Many congregations, schools, businesses and organizations throughout Marin contribute money, time, goods, services to the overall effort of Homeward Bound. This private non-profit has 20 FT employees, and many PT employees.

It is, in many respects, a well-thought out, dynamic, enterprise with deep roots and a highly-respected leadership team. It also fits the modern, post-Reagan model of government staying out of messy social problems and indirectly supporting private non-profits. This arrangement serves another face of modern government: preserving and maintaining the sensitivities of elected officials.

How many homeless persons currently reside in Marin? About 400. Homeward Bound is 40 years old. They are the go-to outfit for every kind of social dysfunction our society in general is reluctant at handling, not just homelessness. They represent one of the best local social movements anywhere. By their own count, they currently handle about 30% of the homeless on the streets of Marin. 30% of the homeless are housed in 40 years. That's the best America can do. Or, at least, the best that California can do.

It's enough to make a person stop and think: what am I getting into? The best program perhaps in all California to support the homeless (among many social needs) houses 3 out of 10 candidates — and that took over 40 years. This model is based upon the deepest mythological belief animating modern Americans: a private non-profit is far better scraping money together than any government action on behalf of its most vulnerable citizens. If a job partially done in 40 years is the best we can do, so be it.

OK, we're sobered up. The government basically frum-frums its way past difficult social solutions because of free market religious ideology, the cult of individualism, fear of asking local citizens to share some of the load because of their reliance on resale potential of their homes, and deference to high-end builders, — all of which concludes in one form or another of "turfing" on homelessness, little to none low-income housing, and whistling past a host of other issues (clean energy, environmental concerns, global warming, etc.) But, housing values are high. That's good for that 20% of the population, right?

Given these political mind-sets, what could a group of citizens who are unelected but wish to be accountable for fixing homelessness do to bring that about in Santa Rosa?

- We see that there are many efforts around the country where local citizens forget politics and join hands to solve a serious challenge that the elected officials cannot or will not tackle. Our own research has indicated to us there are many citizens in Santa Rosa who would dearly love to join a comprehensive, coordinated, and humane effort to solve the homeless challenge, even at some cost to themselves in time and resources.

- We believe the way to engage local citizens is never to hold large meetings, to announce *fait-accompli* "solutions" developed by "experts" that are intended to be imposed on local neighborhoods. Instead, we have developed a plan to cultivate neighbors one at a time to get into the business of renting empty bedrooms, convert garages to small apartments, allow a mini-house to be placed in their backyards to be rented to a low-income worker or a formerly-home-less person.

To unpack the second paragraph above, let's spend a minute explaining our assumptions.

1. The Problem with Large Meetings Regarding Social Challenges.

Change is problematic for lots of folks just because of nature itself. The universe operates on two grand principles: energy and gravity. In the case of homelessness, energy would be represented by the need to house all these folks, and gravity would be represented by the complex of fears felt by some over what such changes might represent to them personally.

Fear is a powerful contagion, and ignorance is its sibling. They combine at large meetings where, in our analogy, the homeless are unnecessarily berated as demons come to ravage a local neighborhood, and any politician fostering such an idea is often characterized as an outside meddler. Most often, under such attacks, such politicians wilt and withdraw their proposals.

On the other hand, our experience and conviction is many citizens do not hold such retrograde views of homelessness. Many folks want solutions. They are sad and embarrassed by seeing the homeless wile away hours and days in unproductive lives on the streets. They do not like the negativity about their own supposed indifference. They do not understand why something humane cannot be done for the homeless and low-income workers in a so-called enlightened era.

What they are waiting for is: (a) a good plan, (b) decent, accountable leadership, and a (c) vision that invites them into the solution as an equal partner.

What we want to do is talk to individual neighbors and put them in the landlord business. We want to help finance the physical changes they might have to underwrite to become landlords. We want to finesse and smooth the permit process with the city. We want to introduce landlords and rental candidates in face-to-face meetings. We want to introduce rental contracts that would be signed by both landlord and client. We want to help guarantee monthly rents. We would share the treatment plan the client might be going through to deal with trauma with selected neighbors.

We would also be recruiting two neighbors on that street to serve as a support team for the landlord and the tenant. We would also assign a trained professional care agent to attend regularly to the needs of the client, and to help the landlord process concerns.

We know how to reach potential landlords through media, congregations, social clubs, senior groups. We know how to conduct small or face-to-face meetings. We know how to ameliorate legitimate fears with facts and on-going support, and how to keep trying.

We also know how to deal with recalcitrant neighbors whose desire to maintain the status quo despite another landlord's basic right to exercise her civil and financial rights if challenged – by quiet, one-on-one meetings, to hold as many of those as it takes.

2. The Kinds of Housing Solutions We Are Proposing and their Process Factors

A. Rental of empty bedroom
- May require a city permit
- Does require a signed contract
- House rules must be agreed to
- Removal of client for cause to be enforced
- Rent most often below market rates
- Clients = low-income workers + homeless
- Two trained neighbors on support team
- All parties networked to non-profit
- Landlord and client may agree to some services in lieu of some rent

B. Placement of mini-house in the back yard

- Non-profit would underwrite part of cost of conversion the building and placement of mini-house w/a 5-year contract allowing non-profit to place approved clients in mini-house under contract.
- Rent would be split by non-profit and landlord.
- At end of 5 years, ownership of mini-house would pass to home-owner
- Permit required.
- All other items listed above would pertain.

C. Conversion of garage to small apartment
  - Non-profit would underwrite part of cost of conversion
  - Rent would accrue to landlord
  - Client = low-income worker or homeless person
  - Non-profit would help select client and supervise contract negotiations
  - Non-profit would recruit and train two neighbors to be in support
  - Non-profit would finesse and smooth permitting process

D. Allowance of right to park vehicle
  - Non-profit would finesse and smooth permit process overnight at local residence
  - Low rental fee would accrue to landlord

3. How Would Non-Profit Find Likely and Willing Landlords?

The new non-profit sees itself as a clearing agency, a go-between, that advertises on TV, print, and social media to residents of Santa Rosa (and Sonoma County), which supplies an array of hard goods and services (mostly gratis) to interested, qualified landlords, to place clients in rentals.

The leads from potential landlords would be answered and qualified by trained volunteers to refine the needs and desires of all parties. The non-profit explains we are in the business of helping place "vetted" clients into existing empty bedrooms, including workers and some formerly homeless persons. If interested in the rental of an empty bedroom, the placement of (paid for) mini-house in the backyard, or the conversion of a garage-to-apartment for rental purposes (partially paid for), the non-profit will set up a qualifying meeting with the landlord to go over all factors and to share a contract for review.

If the landlord is willing to go to contract, the non-profit would introduce a qualified, "VETTED*" candidate at a face-to-face meeting with the landlord.

*VETTED means that the homeless client is assessed by state-certified medical/psychological personnel for the purposes of determining physical, mental, psychological, addictive pathologies, if any; plus, treatment options and regimens as suggested, and their expected duration. A qualified form of this report would be disclosed by permission from the client to the potential landlord with an expert present to explain meaning and expectations.

If the landlord is interested after meeting the client and the expert(s) and is willing to go to contract, the contract will be shared and reviewed by line item so each section can be initialed by both landlord and client.

4. Vendors Required to Build Mini-Houses and Conversion of Garages

The non-profit has identified four builders of mini-houses in the greater Bay Area. In general, we are looking at standard houses, up to 200-300 square feet, featuring a window, step-up porch and entry, door with a lock, built-in storage, insulated, wired for electricity, featuring a chemical bathroom fixture. The mini-house would include standard interior/exterior painting, and come with wheels for ease of placement.

We have seen many kinds of mini-houses with these specifications, and expect to negotiate a cost of under $10,000 per unit. The non-profit would also supply for rental clients a "kit" of standard furniture for the mini-house, plus another kit of clothes.

Regarding vendors for the conversion of garages to apartments, we have identified two vendors we are interested in. Again, for cost purposes, we are very interested in a standard conversion process, not custom jobs. This way, items can be made ahead of time and fitted to local situations. We look to share an initial price to get the project moving but not pay the majority of the cost for garage conversions. We believe a standard conversion of a garage to an apartment can be accomplished for under $25,000 each, including a sink and bathroom.

As we have repeated several times, there is no interest among high-end builders to enter this mini-house or conversion market. Thus, we have sought out a new kind of entrepreneur interested in "cranking out many small houses and conducting standard conversions. "Standard"means just what it implies: each knock-off is 99% the same.

5. What Are the Non-Profit's Expectations Regarding Conversion Rate of New Landlords?

Focus group research found there were at least 3,000 to 7,000 empty bedrooms in the greater Santa Rosa area. At a high-end conversion rate of 7%, an average number we arrived at in all our focus groups, we believe we can rent 400-550 bedrooms over the first five years to approved clients.

We also believe we can place upwards of 300 mini-houses in back-yards over those same 4 years. The rental of the empty bedroom and the rental of the mini-house have different financial assumptions and details of how each would work are explained in a business plan not attached to this book.

We also are very keen on convincing a substantial set of winery owners to consider allowing us to place on their properties upwards of anoth-er 300 mini-houses over the four years after startup. The wineries are in an excellent position to accommodate both the placement of such mini-houses, as many of them already house some workers in this fash-ion, and we feel that with the right plan many of the wineries would also be willing to take the clients under their wing and place them in training programs where they could eventually achieve full-time status as winery workers. This would indeed be a big win for the wineries and certainly for the workers.

Taken together, these three prongs on "clearing-house" matching functions of the non-profit could place at least a 1200 homeless people and some low-income workers in permanent housing in four years.

Extrapolated and projected on Sonoma County, this effort could easily be doubled. Financed properly, and especially based upon continuous assessments of early progress, including the refinement of focused ad-vertising, we believe the effort could be doubled. It is entirely possible to house all of Santa Rosa's homeless population in five years.

6. Doesn't this Plan By-Pass the Proper Authorities of the City and County to House the Indigent and the Low-Income Workers?

It may seem so, but that's a time-phase* problem.
- The town of Santa Rosa and County of Sonoma have no such plans to house the indigent and low-income workers. You can't by-pass what does not exist.
- Why not organize politically and run against the existing supervisors to force the issue. Why not indeed? Because such an effort would be costly, time-consuming, and we may well lose such an election. Running for office to help the homeless and low-income workers has not proven to be a great issue to rally voters so far.
- Instead, we think it would be more useful to assume responsibility for this single issue as a means of providing a model for the city and county to observe and consider as we all move forward. Our primary thrust is to provide housing for those who desperately need it now, today, not ten years from today (f even then). When the supervisors

see a working model to house folks that doesn't disrupt neighbor-hoods, they can get behind it safely. Ultimately, it is the responsibility of the elected officials to fund the indigent, but waiting to date for that leadership has left 2,000 people out in the cold in Santa Rosa, another 1,000 in greater Sonoma county, another 55,000 in Los Angeles, another 77,000 in New York City, and up to a million others across the US.

**Time-phase explained. Our civic effort is ahead of current govern-ment thinking. Waiting for them to assume responsibility for the poor and homeless is a nicety of manners that is irrelevant in the light of their refusal to date to make a plan, show leadership, and ask our citizens to step up to help.

7. How did the non-profit derive its cost estimates for all functions?

Estimating costs for overhead is simple. Estimating costs for mini-houses and refurbishing/converting garages is also simple. But estimating the costs to deliver services to the homeless clients is not easy. Why?

Because *no one in government or the care industry knows what these services cost.*

If you look at what passes as a yearly statement of expenses and in-come from the largest care agency in Santa Rosa, Catholic Charities, you cannot find what anyone would call a balance sheet in the ordinary busi-ness sense. Catholic Charities must know what it pays its employees, what it pays for utilities, what it pays for existing programs, but it doesn't con-duct (at least for publication) time and motion studies to determine what each field activity costs and therefore it doesn't know how to measure effectiveness nor efficiency. Nor do any other care agencies.

As the largest care-agency-recipient of funding from the city, how can such lack of reporting be tolerated?

It is tolerated because both the city and the care agencies have an un-derstanding that while costs are not understood, and because everyone knows these funds are horribly inadequate, neither side will ask embar-rassing questions of the other. Every care agent who performs any such services, such as outreach, assessments, lobbying landlords, etc., knows well that these activities are time-consuming and labor-intensive. What these activities really cost are therefore left an unaddressed topic.

It's not a good way to run a business, is it? The way to finesse one's way past this issue is to not call what you are doing a business. Catholic Charities is a charity organization that allies its aims with the city of Santa Rosa on several fronts, and as long as CC is willing to undertake these services, the city is willing to underwrite some of those costs as long as no one knows the true costs, or is too polite to ask.

Why do we intend to perform time and motion studies to discover costs? Because when we all know what any single activity costs, we can make better-informed judgments about a lot of things, such as:

- Are there better, more efficient ways of performing any activity?
- If any entity is seeking funding from any source, government or private, experience tells us that knowing what all activities cost is very important to everyone involved for general and specific accountability purposes.
- Sooner or later, governments locally and throughout California will be able to see models for how to place homeless persons and low-income workers inside local communities, because the pressure of long commutes, the loss of middle and low-income workers due to negligence regarding housing will become a true crisis, and government will welcome models that understand the process and the costs. Arguments over costs in the absence of hard data are little more than opportunities for posturing. Hard data stops that.

As this book starts out, the truth is most often demonstrated by its effects on the ground. All the king's horses and all the king's men placed less than 100 clients in permanent housing in Santa Rosa in 2018. That effort cost nearly $20 million. Yes, of course a lot of that money went towards maintenance of existing services, reimbursements to the jail and emergency services, but one is permitted to make such an unfair claim because nowhere in the entire city or care agencies can anyone find a single page that explains how each dollar is spent on homelessness, what are the specific outcomes, and how can we improve services. And most important, if we knew what these services cost, we could hold government and the care agencies accountable. If nothing else, that single contribution to the discussion of what to do about homelessness would be worth a lot. (But not as much as housing).

What is the exact relationship between the *care advocates* and the City and County?

This is a fascinating subject. Anyone who attends supervisory meetings open to the public on the topic of homelessness will find the supervisors and city clerks in attendance, a coterie of homeless advocates, and care agency representatives. All possess informed opinions and hard experience to various degrees enabling them to ask good questions and offer sound opinions and proposals for improving the services for the homeless.

Separating out the care agencies for a moment, who are these homeless advocates for the poor and needy citizens among us? For the most part, they are amazing people whose dedication to homelessness issues from deep moral and ethical convictions about care, concern, social awareness, and peaceful societal change. Most are highly educated, unpaid, and spend countless hours attending meetings and performing good works on the streets of their local towns. As a group, they represent the best of who we are.

Are they revolutionaries? Hardly. They do not propose revolution (nor do we), civil unrest, or even (necessarily) political change. Mostly, they believe in the system, and advocate instead for gradualism that is decent, equitable, kind, and loving. Nor are they gadflies, interested in pontificating or hearing their own voices. Instead, through their good works, they represent constant reminders to elected officials, police, and others, that the work they do with the homeless, for one group of untended citizens, is an honorable and needed calling.

Were the Reverend ML King and eminent social activist M. Gandhi revolutionaries?

Not really. In hindsight, both were card-carrying conservatives. How can one say that? Because neither advocated the overthrow of the elected government. Instead, each employed non-violent tactics sewn into social movements that sought to juxtapose the respective cultures' deepest moral and historical values, against *de facto* violations of those values. In King's example, those revered values were the New Testament and the US Constitution, which he brilliantly held up as ideals to be compared with the United States' practice of *de facto* racial segregation. In Gandhi's example, he confronted the British with their own notions of what a free people mean when 100,000 British soldiers tried to maintain control, by force, over 350 million Indian citizens. (Indian population today is over 1.2 billion people).

For the most part, whatever personal political beliefs most of these advocates for justice and equity might hold, they nevertheless operate as statist supporters. They do not, as a rule, organize protests that jam the system, thwart police, or volunteer through their actions to go to jail. Is this unfair, impertinent, or worse, an irrelevant opinion?

I don't think so. While there is no requirement that any of these extraordinary volunteers, many of whom have mastered the details of local government and what is truly going on with the homeless population better than some supervisors – should be reverting to organized demonstrations, etc., to make their points about the lack of proper response to homeless issues large and small. But it is also true that their collective belief in chipping away at the edges of government policy and practice regarding homelessness has hardly moved the needle on this issue in ten years. Any of us must be willing to act in imaginative ways to get this task underway, including incurring the occasional wrath and judgment of those in power who do not seem to be moved, as yet, by all those collective actions that appear to have not pushed them outside their comfort zones.

Is it fair to suggest that the effort to celebrate, honor, and respect these collective efforts despite little progress, should not be our primary focus? Yes. Our focus must be on housing several thousand Olian Byrd's and getting the right kinds of therapies, medications, job training, and associated rehabilitative help now, not in another ten years.

The care agencies, for their part, are not a separate part of the delivery system for services to the poor and homeless, but the integral operational arm of those government-sponsored services, such as they are. Besides not knowing what these services cost (except that their funding is inadequate to the task), the care agencies also do not protest this situation by obstructing meetings, organizing sit-ins, making demands, and all the other well-known tactics of protest and disruption that are designed throw a spotlight on serious societal dysfunctions. Instead, many of the care agencies, founded on long-term religious beliefs, such as perfecting character before providing housing, for one example, appear to prefer to participate in quiet internecine isolation rather than join in common cause with the other care agencies.

The question must be asked: is fixing homelessness about us, or about the homeless? Whose feelings are to be countenanced, listened to, preferred, held as precious?

It is not that this book calls for political opposition to elected officials in Santa Rosa or anywhere else regarding all conditions of the current exercise of their elected power that results in inadequate housing for 80% of the citizens, and little permanent housing at all for 2,000 homeless citizens. But collectively, it does seem that this failure to enlist some active opposition to the status quo on these issues concludes in policies that hardly seem to change for the better. If those working closest to the center of power (advocates and care agencies) do not present a coherent plan to end homelessness, then what are they doing? And if the past is prologue, what is going to happen that will house 2,000 homeless persons, and provide affordable housing for thousands of other low-income citizens of Santa Rosa in the next five, ten years?

Given these realities, are the social advocates and care agencies, along with their good works, unwitting enablers of policies that do not address the needs of the very people they wish to represent?

An impertinent question? I am an observer of the present scene but not morally-superior. Nothing that is being currently done in Santa Rosa, or any other town in California, or America, is anything but the product of the longest-term gradualist agenda, activities that could be viewed by some as luxuries for those of us who can go home nightly to a decent meal and a warm bed, while 2,000 Olian Byrds pull their greasy tarps a bit tighter as the fall winds sweep down on them.

What position does the non-profit you contemplate occupy in the political context you describe above?

The non-profit we contemplate makes the following assumptions:

- The locally-elected officials in Santa Rosa and the County of Sonoma are not presently committed to the elimination of homelessness by offering any kind of permanent housing to all the homeless in the near term. Neither are either bodies committed to changing the rules that allow high-end builders to continue to dominate the discussion on what kinds of houses are built (90%+ high end) or to evade the topic altogether by paying a nominal fee to the town to by-pass the soft rule that allows such a dismissal.
- The care agencies do not know what their own services cost, nor do they publish accounting reports that are recognizable regarding outcomes. They lobby for funding from government as individual entities instead of joining together as a unified voice, and essentially are in the business of perpetual processing, not ending, homelessness.
- The volunteer care advocates historically do not seem disposed to challenge the status quo on homelessness as much as to try to improve the situation by gradualist methodologies.
- The various police departments who act as camp-clearers, serial arrest agents of recalcitrant homeless offenders, garbage disposers of the flotsam collected by the homeless, appear to hate these exercises to nowhere. There does not seem to be any alternative, however, for along with bromides from elected officials about how they are working hard to provide housing that never seems to appear, the police must also field troops to clear homeless encampments to placate local businesses that are frustrated and anxious about homeless people annoying paying customers.
- The State of California, dominated by educated, politically liberal office-holders, does not seem yet inclined, confident, or self-empowered to address the true housing crisis throughout the state for 80% of its citizens, nor for the 18% of the nation's homeless who happen to reside in California, for fear of offending the wealthy 20% of California voters who dominate the political (donor) class and business interests.
- No entity, elected or not, seeks the underlying hows and whys

neighborhoods so often reject proposals to house some homeless or low-income workers locally. Dealing only with these reactions, most-to-all such proposals to house the homeless die still-born.

FOUNDING PRINCIPALS

- Private funding (not governmental) by-passes the entire political and entrenched establishment thinking and practice on homelessness and low-income housing. While government is not the enemy, a fish in water does not know it's in water until it is out of water. Changing that water is not exhibition of some presumed superiority but an act of desperation based upon these realities. The work of this non-profit is to provide a model, not in perpetuity, but first to help the home-less, and secondly to provide a model about costs, effectiveness, and purposeful housing now for 2,000 homeless and hundreds of low-in-come workers.
- We intend to employ selected care agencies to carry out many of the street-based activities they currently perform and are trained for but on a different payment basis that measures these activities to discov-er what they truly cost and to also discover hidden efficiencies, if they exist.
- We intend to employ existing (and willing) local homeless advocates to help administer our company, especially those who are trained in senior positions and who demonstrate experience and knowledge in the complex areas we seek.
- The police are not the enemy. On the contrary, while they work most-ly at the behest of city officials and business people, as is usually the case, we believe many of the police personnel would be very open to a more humane treatment of the homeless if they were shown ways and means to do this.
- We have a special and deep interest in engaging a small army of trained volunteers to operate as neighborhood organizers. This ac-tivity, thus far the third rail of political reality, is essential to a peaceful means to integrate the homeless and low-income workers back into local neighborhoods. However, we believe the means we employ to do this sets us apart from heretofore heavy-handed government proposals on such matters.

Generally speaking, our operational principals do not spell out *"a pox on all your houses."* Yes, we are frustrated with the stasis regarding home-lessness and housing in general from all quarters, and we do not have much confidence that much in positive substance can result in the next ten years from those quarters unless they adopt very different methods. But we do not disdain government, the police, the care agencies, and street activists. Instead, we believe a short-cut to success that could house 2,000 homeless and hundreds of low-income workers in 5 years is possible and achievable by going around the status quo but without disdaining those actors, as a means of deploying a working model that could be studied and, where successful, perhaps modified and copied elsewhere.

Narrative Explanation of How Leads for Landlords to Rent Empty Bedrooms and/or Allow Placement of Mini-Houses or Garage Conversions to Apartments.

The non-profit contracts with a professional, experienced media production company to generate a series of 30 and 60 second video ads which will be aired in low-cost rotations at cost-effective flight-times during a 24-hour cycle with the charge to call an 800 number if the respondent wants further information about how to become a landlord in one of several special programs.

Similar ads will also be prepared for social media and print forums.

All such call-leads will be processed by trained responders who qualify the potential landlord and set up a meeting to answer further questions.

MODELS FOR ACTION

- **Rental of an empty bedroom, use of bathroom, use of kitchen**. Rental at below-market rate of $800/mo. If the landlord is a senior or disabled person, arrangements can be made to establish a series of services to be performed by the client-tenant in lieu of some rent, including errands, shopping, driving, cleaning, outdoor work, etc. Person-to-person meeting(s) are arranged to introduce a "vetted" client and landlord, supervised by non-profit personnel. A standard rental contract is introduced and reviewed. House rules are expressed and if agreed to, incorporated into the contract. A summarized review of any on-going treatment services required by the client will be shared (the essence of a medical condition w/o unnecessarily invading client privacy). If all is agreed to, contracts are signed.
- **Placement of a standard non-profit-sponsored mini-house in back yard**. The landlord would agree to permit the non-profit to place a client of its choosing in the mini-house, pursuant to the above filtered disclosures and assurances regarding the client's physical and mental conditions.

  Below-market rent ($500-$800/mo) will be charged by the non-profit, but split with the landlord at 50% each. The mini-house also comes with a kit of furniture and a clothes package. A contract reflecting house/property rules would be reviewed and signed. An agreement is struck between the non-profit and the property-owner that after 5 years of this arrangement, the ownership of the mini-house will be turned over to the property-owner to use as she wishes. City permit required for installation.

- **Garage conversion to a rental apartment**. Requires a city permit, which would be facilitated by the non-profit. Non-profit encourages such conversions by offering to pay the first $5,000 of costs for the conversion, as well as to help arrange financing for the balance via favorable terms from a friendly bank. The landlord would agree to consider clients provided first by the non-profit and for a period of three years, to offer such rentals at 60% of market rates (locally, in the $1,000/mo. range).

These three housing programs answer several of the essential questions raised in our focus groups which sit just beneath the objections of so many local citizens who resist governmental imposition of so-called housing solutions for homeless people that always seem to impinge on low-income neighborhoods:

1. The ads can be answered by anyone, anywhere, from any neighborhood. We do not choose the landlord; she chooses herself.
2. Our non-profit helps the home-owner become a landlord and gain income, allowing many such landlords to age in place with additional financial security.
3. Our approach allows the local landlord some control over the selection of the client, instead of being cast into a "victim" position by impositions of large building proposals that instantly coalesce resistance.

Choice, income, control: smells like America.

VOLUNTEERS

How Are They Recruited, What Do They Do, How Are They Trained?

A cadre of volunteers lies at the heart of what the non-profit intends to accomplish in Santa Rosa and Sonoma County with the homeless and low-income workers.

Volunteers are not a strategy to lessen overhead costs but an essential means to utilize the pent-up good will observed throughout the city of Santa Rosa with many citizens who are frustrated with the *de facto* failure of the city to deal humanely and effectively with the housing and homeless crises. We are not imagining this good will; we have observed it up close; we have talked to many people who have indicated to us that if an organization were to come along with a good plan, some dedicated leadership, adequate funding for a consistent effort over an extended period, and especially with the goal of housing the homeless and as many low-income workers as possible now, they would be interested in helping as a volunteer.

Individuals in our non-profit have extensive experience recruiting and training individuals for a wide variety of activities. For this effort, we contemplate the following:

- The first means of recruiting is to call on a wide list of individuals we have already identified to join our effort. We would also place print ads locally as well as social networking to attract others; the second is to recruit inside houses of worship, senior and social groups.
- The tasks for volunteers that are planned include the following: (1) responding and qualifying leads from potential landlords; (2) setting up meetings with potential landlords; (3) supervising those meetings, including follow-on meetings with both client and landlord; (4) introducing formal, standard contracts including codicils reflecting agreed-to house rules and securing signatures.
- Helping clients "move in," get settled, especially those occupying mini-houses with its furniture considerations.
- Helping to coordinate follow-on care protocols for appropriate clients with medical personnel, and helping to coordinate rides to and from appointments.
- A very important service to be performed by volunteers is securing neighborhood support for the client and landlord with at least two close-by neighbors. These support neighbors are identified in the first instance by the landlord herself and afterwards by contacting co-church members to the landlord that may live within a short distance.

NEIGHBORHOOD SUPPORT TEAMS

What is it the neighborhood support teams do for the landlord and client?

1. They provide a first line of response when anything goes amiss. They operate as friends of both landlord and client. They try to ameliorate such difficulties in embryo stage. The non-profit will also train these neighbors to not just follow common sense but know how to identify certain problems and responses, including calling the non-profit and or medical or other professionals to respond, if warranted.
2. The volunteers play an enormous role with other neighbors by talking quietly when and if there are questions raised about who the new tenant is, what neighbors might expect, and even how neighbors can help. The volunteers are neighbor-hood peace-makers.

With volunteers, the non-profit addresses a fundamental ethical mandate of encouraging neighborhood members to be part of the solution for homeless and the housing crisis. Placement of clients one-by-one inside neighborhoods ought by itself not be disruptive, or threatening to housing prices, or a reason for anxiety and stress among close-by neighbors, but in case any of these questions are raised, our volunteers are in a perfect position to use such occasions as a learning/teaching opportunity. In this way, two objectives are achieved: the client gets placed back where he belongs — inside neighborhoods — and the neighbors find themselves where they belong, at peace with reconciling with neighbors who had been hitherto cast away.

Volunteers are essential for this non-profit to thrive and for our objectives to house 2,000 homeless people to occur.

Volunteers are essential for Santa Rosa as a city to be at peace with itself on this moral crisis in our midst.

THE WINE INDUSTRY'S BIG ROLE

"We have a crisis," cried one of the participants in a recent meeting of employers (Business Journal, July, 2109)). Because of all the aforesaid economic determinants, — housing too expensive for 80% of the local workers, a low jobless rate, 25% of older workers (125,000) expected to retire within the next five years in Sonoma, — many employers, including the winery owners, are facing a dire situation. They can't fill at least 15,000 job openings right now, and the underlying conditions listed above do not portend that this situation is expected to get any better soon. This includes the wine growers, who are hundreds of workers short of a full complement. In addition, stable workers who are local are being squeezed out of rentals. Many teachers and nurses, for example, travel from places like Fairfield and Vallejo, a good hour and a half away from Santa Rosa, to get to their jobs.

Sonoma County boasts almost 1800 vintners, most modest-sized ranches, ten well over several thousand acres under cultivation. Sonoma produces 6% of all California wine. The industry employs thousands of workers, from hospitality greeters in tasting rooms, managers, workers who operate and maintain machinery, and many field-workers who tend to the vines and bring in the harvest.

Seasonal field workers used to be the rule in California wine fields, many of them migrating especially for the harvest. However, the current manufactured crisis at the US border with Mexico is putting a serious strain on such migrations, and therefore the readiness of the wineries to bring in their harvests. As a result, many are looking to find machinery that can harvest grapes, but the current state and cost of that machinery still leaves much to be desired.

In short, the Sonoma wine industry needs workers. We have them.

Our non-profit wants to place mini-houses (paid for by the non-profit) on their properties, where many such wineries already support some kinds of permanent housing with bathrooms and showers, and then enter agreements where vetted workers would be apprenticed for a period to the growers and receive job-training. The hope would be that as the workers learn and demonstrate over a period that they are trustworthy and industrious, the wine managers would hire them full time at the current rates.

What a wonderful thing this would be for the worker to receive permanent housing and the emotional stability of a training program which could lead to a full-time job! What a wonderful thing this would be for the wineries to not only get some of their labor needs met, but to play such an active role in the redemption of their fellow human beings!

If only 100 formerly homeless and low-income workers were placed in wineries in this manner over a several-year period, and the entire process was audited and noted for all its benefits and mistakes, it could prove one of the best ways to rescue capitalism gone deaf and blind to human need immediately in its midst.

FUNDING: WHERE IS IT?

Look around California and the other states: where is the funding for homelessness, such as it is, coming from?

If we can admit what our eyes tell us, we all know that whatever the funding is from the federal government, the states, and local communities, it is seriously inadequate to the task. How do we know this? Because we don't have to read any more of the thousand reports written every year about how the homeless crisis stays the same or gets worse, do we? Since most of these reports also fail to account for the underlying causes of homeless, which this book does do, the mountain of reports amount to little more than academic exercises, voices shouting into an empty canyon.

No, if you want to see financial action on the homeless front in today's America, you need to talk to our billionaires, and large corporations.

Locally, please note this:
- Kaiser Permanente his announced a fund of $200 million to fight homelessness country-wide.
- Wells Fargo has announced a similar $100 million fund to fight homelessness.
- Cisco has dedicated $50 million to the cause.

- As listed above, a billionaire in San Francisco has raised $100 million to battle homelessness, but he thinks this plan will only settle 1,000 homeless over a five-year period inside San Francisco.
- The federal government estimates that to place every homeless person in permanent housing in the US would require an initial $2.7 billion and not be completed until 2037.

We must remember the underlying dynamics of homelessness:
1. Preventing homelessness is the best stopgap to its growth. Current housing policy in California is working against this prospect.
2. Providing shelters delays but does not end homelessness.
3. Coming to grips with a housing policy that does not accommodate the needs of 80% of California's population (32 million people) is not on the horizon.
4. No one is seriously talking about how to engage neighborhoods in the homeless solution.

So, in desperation, activists give up on government, and turn to billionaires and big companies. Can these folks save us?

Perhaps those who engage with the very wealthy to fund homeless projects should not look a gift-horse in the mouth. If the billionaires want to help, no matter what their real motivations, why not jump on that?

Here is what we have decided: we are looking for wealthy partners, at least at first, because we deeply feel that our energy trying to convince elected officials to assume responsibility will cost us all our time but guarantee no certain outcome. Our constituency is not local government; it is the homeless and their immediate needs. However, we also are not interested in being part of a public relations effort. If one should make the first assumption that billionaires and wealthy companies have motives are pure and decent, it is also OK to maintain some objective detachment from what could devolve into a PR effort.

We say this because we are committed to transparency. We intend to make our progress, or lack of progress, public information all the way through the process.

How else can we build trust? How can we gain the confidence with local neighbors that we are acting as honest brokers, not trying to change their neighborhoods in a *sub rosa* manner to foist some progressive social improvement project?

We just want to house homeless persons and low-income workers. We don't want to win philosophical arguments. So, if we cannot engage wealthy funders with a realistic and achievable plan, show consistent and competent leadership, field a large volunteer cadre to address a neighborhood engagement plan, then what is it wealthy funders would be interested in?

Our point is that independent funding allows us to get to work, report our results, house the unsheltered, engage neighbors, train volunteers, without having to beg local and state government in a 30-year effort to do the right thing. Sooner or later, however, government has to step up with proper funding. It is our hope and belief that seeing a working model, leadership, local support, and what such activities cost, will prompt them to act. In any case, the local homeless would have been housed.

We believe those wealthy individuals and corporations who truly want to make a difference for the homeless will be found. Maybe some of the readers of this book will be among them.

We have written a comprehensive business plan and completed all the finances for a five-year effort in one American city, Santa Rosa, CA, that would house 2,000 individuals presently sleeping on our streets, including some low-income workers. The plan does not include multi-story buildings that would serve little more than targets for loud resistance. We believe we can house all these folks right now with available housing that is right under our noses.

What would this cost, according to our plan? Under $20 million.

To put that in perspective, to re-pave a one-mile section of any road in Santa Rosa costs about $5 million. Santa Rosa needs both things: repaved roads, and housing for the homeless. You can guess which one gets done.

18% of all the homeless persons in America reside in California, a state that likes to see itself as the leader in progressive reform. Homelessness, in our opinion, is the first among equal issues in need of reform from malign neglect to benign respect. Come join us.

SUMMARY OF OLIAN BYRD COALITION PLAN

Summary of the Olian Byrd Coalition to End Homelessness in Santa Rosa and its Business Plan Fundamentals

- We are a non-profit dedicated to one thing: housing all the current homeless people in Santa Rosa in five years from start-up and creating a working model for export elsewhere, if desirable.
- We are a clearing-house-matching-company that puts landlords and clients together for no fees.
- We engage existing care agencies personnel as professional workers who perform outreach to clients, assessments, other wrap-around services for clients.
- We enter relationships with mini-house builders to produce standardized small houses and garage conversions for rentals to homeless and low-income workers at below-market rates.
- We enter into a strategic-partner relationship with the Sonoma Vintners Association to place mini-houses on their properties and encourage them to train clients to become FT workers.
- We locate, train, supervise, and reinforce a large volunteer force to help organize our effort in local neighborhoods.
- We perform time and motion studies of all activities to understand and derive accurate assumptions about what every single activity costs so we can report these numbers to all interested parties and be held accountable by funders, government, and the public.

WHAT ABOUT AFTERCARE FOR CLIENTS?

Interviews with care agencies who deal directly every day with all the services required for formerly homeless clients operate on two assumptions: (1) half the clients will require an array of services for an extended period, and (2) those services can cost up to $7500 per client. We assume the same. Therefore, our non-profit will help underwrite those costs, which, averaged over all clients, will average $3750 per client over a five-year period. This topic is treated with greater detail in our business plan.

PART V: WHAT COULD GO WRONG?

(A) Any honest attempt to out together a business plan needs to account for doubts, concerns, and as far as any of us can, anticipate untoward events.

It's entirely possible that despite our best efforts at explaining the root causes of homelessness, and developing strategies to work around those root causes to house 2,000 people in one small city, we may nevertheless fail to impress funders.

This author, among others affiliated with our effort, has started several companies and had to raise significant capital to get them up and running. While all those companies were for-profit, thus explaining the obvious interest those funders had in a financial upside from their investment, there is much in common among funders when it comes to reading and believing in a business plan, even if the effort is for a non-profit enterprise.

A non-profit needs to demonstrate that its argument for funding is based upon more than doing good; it needs to show that its existence fulfills some important niche that is being unaddressed by other contemporary means. We believe that America, and our federal, state and local governments, are not paying much attention to a housing disaster brewing right in front of their eyes. Or, if they are paying some attention, they are politically paralyzed from responding with practical solutions.

We expect to solicit financial help from funders by inviting them into the process so they can add their experience and unique perspectives to our overall effort. One would hope that if we can demonstrate cost-effective solutions to permanent housing for low-income workers and homeless persons in local neighborhoods without social disruption, that prospect might prove attractive to funders, especially if such solutions prove transportable to other communities.

(B) While this book does not hesitate to directly or indirectly implicate all the current players – all government levels, the care agencies, (much less) the social advocates who do so much for the poor and homeless might also act as possible enablers of the current micro-movement on housing and homeless. How then would our non-profit work with these same players after implying as such?

It may seem beside the point, but describing a situation does not necessarily serve as an indictment of ill will or incompetence of those players. Secondly, funding has a powerful influence on any such bruised feelings. Like a kaleidoscope that suddenly clicks into focus, funding has a way of focusing the mind to the task at hand. We intend to hire several experienced, knowledgeable social advocates currently operating in Santa Rosa as executives in our company; in addition, we intend to contract with several existing care agency personnel to perform important functions regarding outreach to prospective clients, comprehensive assessments to determine mental, physical and psychological profiles of clients, among other functions. We need these important people to help us. We believe they will join us.

It could be a more delicate matter to impress and engage some Supervisors who suddenly are made aware that a public-private, non-profit with funding independent of the city and county is operating as an unelected but accountable coalition of local citizens to directly address a major social issue without asking the city and county for permission.**

On the other hand, there are permit and legal issues that must be met and approved by the town and county, so we intend to invite the local supervisors into a joint effort that will promise and deliver on the following:

- Expediting permits for mini-houses and garage upgrades to apartments are ideas that everyone can value. If the supervisors of Santa Rosa find building housing for low-income workers and homeless persons too politically or financially daunting, our solutions may prove more acceptable and achievable, thus streamlining the permitting process might be something they could accomplish with little political cost.
- We believe most of the supervisors are deeply interested in solutions to housing and homelessness. Inasmuch as our model is a transparent effort, as we intend to regularly publish results, costs, and methodology studies on how we approach neighbors in small meetings, etc., this information should be of high interest to folks who wish to run for office.

(C) Some clients, possibly suffering from long-term, unaddressed mental disorders, may be able to rent an empty bedroom or mini-house but act out in ways that alarm the landlord or otherwise prove too difficult to manage even through the auspices of care agents assigned to the client.

Removing a person from a rental is a legal process that must be followed in the State of California. However, certain behaviors can be included in the rental contract that, if initiated or prolonged without appropriate fixes, could conclude in the client being removed by the non-profit (but placed in another such room or mini-house). We acknowledge we are in new territory here and we will be guided by obtaining law, all rights inuring to all parties, expert opinion, good sense, and a willingness to solve such challenges on behalf of all stakeholders.

(D) We discover our research data, or our evolved, close-up approach to dealing with individuals instead of large assemblies, is possibly over-valued and our numbers for placements are not being achieved at predicted values.

Revision of basic assumptions is always more than an option in a start-up, it's a necessity. Success in doing so requires a reciprocal trust among funders, board members, and the operational executives.

(E) Can a small start-up in a small western city truly accomplish something that has so far eluded huge cities and tiny towns – eliminating homelessness in a five-year period?

We believe we as team have probably spent more time doing the kind of social and demographic analysis than most start-ups in our business. We know we do not share many of the assumptions that drive most such efforts in homelessness, such as offering another version of shelters as our solution, or trying to get builders and politicians together to build large installations to house many hundreds of individuals in need of permanent but below-market rentals.

We feel the only chance we have to change minds along with the immediate goals of housing needful individuals, is to work inside small knots of sympathetic folks so we have an opportunity to build community organically. We don't see those kinds of opportunities being discussed currently among builders, elected officials, or towns.

We hope and believe, as mature, experienced individuals, that we are cognizant of the pitfalls of hubris and self-infatuation, the love of ideas for their own sake, and overly optimistic, or pessimistic, views of ourselves or our neighbors. We don't have to convince everyone to win the day. In Santa Rosa, among its 180,000 inhabitants, we need to convince 2,000 (1.6%) citizens to open their hearts and offer empty bedrooms, backyards, or garages to house a homeless person or a low-income worker.

That is a real challenge, but we think it's doable. And we think there are many Santa Rosa citizens who will join with us.

Consideration of resistance from supervisors who might view such an in-dependently-funded, street-based, non-profit organization proposing to enlist a portion of the public to themselves help solve the homeless cri-sis, — not as a humanitarian impulse, but an organized political effort to embarrass them or challenge their authority?

This possibility is not lost on us. However, we ourselves do not intend to do to the supervisors what some of them have tried to do on sever-al occasions to poor neighborhoods: impose some kind of *fait accompli* "terrific solution" on them without any preparation, advance information of their intentions. If we are successful raising capital to fund our non-profit, we would seek meetings with supervisors to engage them in the details of our plan, and to ask them to help us by streamlining the permit process, perhaps sitting on our executive advisory council, setting up periodic dates for us to report our progress, and so on.

The supervisors are not the enemy. They want solutions to the homeless crisis as we do. We want to engage them in our effort.

WHO BENEFITS FROM SCARCITY OF HOUSING?

Finally, a big question raised earlier but not answered until now. Who benefits from the Scarcity of housing? Roman politicians asked this question, "Who Benefits?" 2,000 years ago. It's still one of the keys to understanding how statist politics work anywhere, anytime. The answer is as follows:

The direct beneficiaries of scarce housing are the wealthy. Keeping housing scarce and expensive solves a lot of social issues for the wealthy. Since the top 10% have the means to negotiate the complexity of high-end housing, and all the rest do not, their neighborhoods can be tightly controlled to keep out all who cannot negotiate those complexities. If these unwritten but operative policies indirectly reinforce racist housing practices, lock immigrants out of local public schools, consign workers and middle class folks to 90 minute commutes to and from work, constitute obstructionist inertia to government to improve mass transportation, and thus are primarily organized around the preservation of their neighborhood as a haven from riffraff concerns, well, aren't they just living the American dream?

You know, that dream that says if you want into this neighborhood, start your own software company.

If the next great wave of economic reform and justice is just around the corner, hooray!

If the next wave of the melting of hard hearts enabling people of privilege to welcome the poor and homeless into their neighborhoods is finally at hand, hooray!

If the State of California is finally ready to embrace housing for low-income workers and the homeless despite their donor-class ferociously resisting such impulses, hooray!

If the City of Santa Rosa and the County of Sonoma are finally ready to embrace a housing policy to build thousands of houses and apartments for low-income workers and the homeless despite the implicit political understanding among the elected officials and their sponsors who really count – business and the wealthy — who insist that such changes would threaten the ambiance of their lovely neighborhoods, and therefore should proceed at a snail's pace so this place of natural beauty, although enjoyed by less and less, might be preserved, ... well, gosh, hooray!

BUT, should these beliefs, values, political networks, implied under-standings, should not result in any substantive changes for low-income housing in the next five to ten years, or decades, or half a century, then perhaps a group of local citizens can revert to another, just as old, and just as powerful (if not used as often) belief: *We the people, in order to form a more perfect union, must do the work that needs be done, ourselves.*

Not insurrection. Not disruption. Just a large group of folks who see the need, see some reasonable solutions, and are willing to put a lot of time into an effort to house a few thousand fellow citizens.

WHAT'S OUR CALL TO ACTION TO THE READERS OF THIS BOOK?

How else do you honestly think this work can be done, given what we all know about past practices, beliefs, on the part of those who benefit from the status quo?

This book is not an intellectual exercise. We need to get busy. You need to help us.

POST SCRIPT

The Alligator and the Frog

Everyone will remember the story about the alligator and the frog. The latter, of course a little chap, hops down to the river, eager to get to the other side to greet family and food again. But it's a huge and deep river, full of predators just waiting for a little frog to try to swim his way across.

At the water's edge, the little frog spies an alligator sunning himself. Does the giant reptile even notice the frog, or is his seeming obliviousness just an act?

"Wow, that's a mighty stream. I could never cross that."

The alligator opens a blinked eye. "Yup, it's pretty deep, and dangerous, too. But you're in luck; I happen to be going over there just now, and you can hitch a ride."

The frog may have been small, but he wasn't stupid. "That's very nice of you, but I fear by reputation you will eat me as soon as I hop aboard."

"No, no, little frog. First, there's nothing much to you, so you're not worth the meal. Second, I'm full. Third, I'm going over there anyway, so if you want a ride, just hop on my head and you'll be there lickety-split." And the alligator started to waddle towards the river's edge.

Watching his possible ride launch itself towards the water, the little frog went into a panic, talking to himself against his experience and intuition that maybe this giant alligator could be trusted, maybe his statements were sincere, and if he didn't act right now, maybe the ride would disappear.

So, he jumped aboard the alligator's snout, moved to his flat head, and out they ventured into the deep and raging river.

About 30 yards out into the river, the alligator suddenly flipped his head; the little frog was cast into the void above for just a moment, then settled down again right inside the alligator's huge mouth. Just before he was to be sliced in those fearsome teeth, he croaked to the alligator: 'How could you. You promised me you wouldn't do this."

"I know," said the alligator. "I just can't help myself."

Here are some things to consider when assessing whether a group of local citizens can actually take on an abiding social problem and try to solve it:

1. "Hope" is an illusion. There is only doing. We can have hope for the homeless, or we can house them, now, together.
2. People and institutions who benefit from access to and control over

how the economy works are not disposed, like the alligator, to anything but what has benefited them forever. Bankers do not ask to regulate themselves. Wall Street will not voluntarily submit to financial regulation; on the contrary, it's entire history is one of "exploiting the given rules of the day" to the greatest advantage. The poor and homeless have no natural representation in government. Congress, no matter what party is in power, has few people there who are working advocates for the poor and homeless.

These are not the words of embitterment, but cold realism. We are not disgusted with the system, but wish to invoke its deepest spiritual roots, including self-empowerment. There are no free rides across this river to housing the homeless from those agents who constantly betray trust issues. It's just us. It's a freeing thought. It's about us, the homeless and the rest of us.

We build our own little boat, try to house all the little frogs, and get to the other side, together. Let's get going.

ABOUT THE AUTHOR

Terry Rowan is an entrepreneur and educator with wide-experience in start-ups, community organizing, media, and political campaigning. Since 2010, he has written four books, with another novel due for publication in the fall, 2019 (all available at Amazon). He lives in Santa Rosa, California, with his wife, and close to some of his grandchildren.

CONTACT INFORMATION

Interested in more information, a business plan and
financials presentation?

Contact: terryrow1@comcast.net